# Breakaway Careers

## The Self-Employment Resource for Freelancers, Consultants, and Corporate Refugees

By
Bill Radin

CAREER PRESS
180 Fifth Avenue
P.O. Box 34
Hawthorne, NJ 07507
1-800-CAREER-1
201-427-0229 (outside U.S.)
FAX: 201-427-2037

## BREAKAWAY CAREERS

ISBN 1-56414-121-7, $12.95

Cover design by The Gottry Communications Group, Inc.

Printed in the U.S.A. by Book-mart Press

To order this title by mail, please include price as noted above, $2.50 handling per order, and $1.00 for each book ordered. Send to: Career Press, Inc., 180 Fifth Ave., P.O. Box 34, Hawthorne, NJ 07507.

Or call toll-free 1-800-CAREER-1 (Canada: 201-427-0229) to order using VISA or MasterCard, or for further information on books from Career Press.

**Library of Congress Cataloging-in-Publication Data**

Radin, Bill.
    Breakaway careers / by Bill Radin.
        p.    cm.
    Includes index.
    ISBN 1-56414-121-7 : $12.95
    1. Self-employed. 2. New business enterprises. I. Title.
HD8036.R33    1994
    658'.041--dc20
                                                                94-3107
                                                                CIP

# Acknowledgments

I wish to thank those who helped make *Breakaway Careers* possible, including my family; and all the dedicated professionals in the employment and self-employment industries: Peter Yessne, Richard Belous, H. B. Gelatt, Audrey Freedman, Andrea Kay, Peter Leffkowitz, Danny Cahill, Paul Hawkinson, Nancy Schretter, Martin Yate, Bob Cowan, Michael Zatzick, Tim Moffitt, Mary Lou Rimsky and Bill Vick.

Special thanks to Betsy Sheldon, Joyce Hadley, Mike Baird, Larry Wood, Ellen Scher, Ron Fry, Bob and Larry Newman, Sally Anne McCartin, Heather Olsen, Oscar Collier, Scott Woelfel, Mark Bartolomeo, Dorothy Rosa, Tom Laskey, Jean Peters, Bonnie Krstolic, Bill Moss, Chris Mather, Rick Oseas, Lynn Sontag, Bill Gwynne, Pat Kelly, Bob Roetker, David Wolfe, Bert Holtje, Chuck Weideman, Ken Kresge, Ray Lange, John and Bonnie Helgeson, Burt Sugar, Scott and Maggie Woelfel, the Parr family, Hope Newman, Nancy Aldrich, Andrea Brown, Bill Fahy, Bill Zabriskie and Kent James.

Heartfelt thanks to my wife, Ruth, and stepdaughter Randi Lorber, for your patience and encouragement.

*Breakaway Careers* is dedicated
to the memory of Jimmy McGary.

*Name no one man.*

# Contents

## Chapter 4

### Boot Camp for Breakaways

The verbatim career/Learning to sail alone/Bona fide courses of study/Unwritten restrictions apply/The college of breakaway science/Hunk of the month club/The bookworm solution/Other publications/How to SCORE a mentor/Don't leave home without it/Before you take the leap

## Chapter 5

### Creating a Dynamite Business Plan

A tangible yardstick of commitment/Screenplay or surgery?/Standing the test of time/Goals and objectives/Your best estimate of success/The twenty questions/A plan, not a prediction/A strategy that wears well

## Chapter 6

### Raising the Seed Money You Need

Candid correspondence between a super entrepreneur and his financial advisor, regarding subjects such as parental loans, government grants, private investment capital, bank loans, home equity loans, private stock offerings, venture capital firms, niche financiers, consumer finance companies, investor advisor firms, plastic lines of credit and good old-fashioned bartering.

## Chapter 7

### If It's All the Same, What's In a Name?

Beyond the birds and bees/The name is the game/Names only a mother could love/Name duplications/Anteaters and gunslingers

## Chapter 8

### Cost Containment, Image Control and Legal Self-Protection

A breakaway, not a dilettante/Capital punishment/Heavy metal yuppie/A man to remember/Home is where the action is/A worthwhile trade-off/Diffusing the home office stigma/The media that takes the message/To lease or not to lease/Beware of the software dog/Stationery on a shoe-string/Friendly advice from a direct competitor/Desktop options/A valuable and versatile tool/Corporation, partnership or sole proprietorship?/Limiting your liabilities and losses/The health insurance dilemma

consumer markets/Calculating fees/3. The seminar trade/Seminar topics/Forget Toastmasters, this is a business/Books, reports and videotapes

# Introduction

---◆---

# Take This Job and Leave It

---◆---

Four years ago, I walked away from a management position with a $400 million corporation and never looked back.

Gone are the benefits, the perks, the promotions and the fancy offices.

Also gone are the boring meetings, the cutthroat office politics, the 60-minute commutes and the migraine headaches.

I like my new lifestyle better.

My office now is a converted second-floor bedroom above the two-car garage in my Santa Fe home. My commute time is approximately seven seconds, or more precisely, the time it takes me to carry a cup of coffee from the kitchen up the stairs to my office every morning.

Usually, I'm at my desk by around 8:30 or 9:00. Of course, the cat has gotten there first, but Keeper's pretty accommodating and lets me share it with him.

Admittedly, the atmosphere at the office is pretty relaxed. Although I meet with a dozen senior-level corporate executives every day, my attire ranges from moderately casual to *majorly grunged* (as Randi, my teenage stepdaughter, would say), depending on my mood. But it hardly matters, since nearly all my meetings are conducted over the phone. On the rare occasions when I need to visit with a client in person, I simply dust off one of the pinstripe suits languishing in the hall closet since my departure from dress-for-success America, and no one's the wiser.

As I sit and watch the seasons change from my suburban vantage point, I wonder how I ever survived the pressure of the high-rise corporate world; and I think of how lucky I am that the recent advances in technology have given me the opportunity to lead such a fulfilling life. In the last four years, I've had more "jobs" than most people in previous generations ever dreamed of having in a lifetime. Thanks to the telephone, the fax machine, the personal computer and an assortment of electronic peripherals, I now wear several complementary and free-standing occupational hats, each of my own choosing.

I have a breakaway career, and I love it.

## The phenomenon

Many of my friends also have breakaway careers. They work as market researchers, songwriters, massage therapists, software specialists, interim executives, cost control experts, freelance artists, literary agents, career counselors, public relations consultants, accountants, attorneys—and the list goes on.

The fact is, breakaways like my friends and I represent the fastest-growing segment of the employment picture—an estimated one-third of the total job market in the United States, according to the National Planning Association in Washington, D.C. Also known by economists as the *contingent work force*, breakaways are those people who make their living on a self-employed, contract, temporary or part-time basis.

By the year 2000, it's predicted that those in the "core" work force (that is, those who owe their allegiance to a single, full-time employer) will actually be in the *minority*. Everyone else will have broken away.

The breakaway phenomenon is a direct result of powerful social, economic and technological forces in today's global society, in which the very concept of "work" has been completely redefined. Take the notion of job security, for example. It no longer matters to an employer how many years of faithful service you've logged.

9

What's important from the perspective of the company is simply the quality of the work you provide, pure and simple.

Of course, quality is a two-way street. For example, you may not care a whit that your company presented you with a bronze plaque at the annual Christmas party. What you're interested in is the daily challenge at your desk and the freedom to balance your personal and professional goals.

As the industrialized nations shift from a captive to a contingent organizational framework, people on both sides of the payroll are beginning to look at their work relationships objectively. And they're discovering that, increasingly, there are no "employers" or "employees;" there are only *work needers* and *work providers*. Anymore, as long as you can do the piece of work required and satisfy the person who writes the check, you've got yourself a livelihood.

## Cocktail party protocol

My own career is a classic example.

After breaking away from the big corporation, I founded a highly specialized executive search firm, which represents the foundation of my business. As long as I provide a valuable brokering service to both work needers and work providers (in this case, job-seekers and employers), my business will flourish.

However, I also have several secondary streams of income. For example, a few years back, I developed a seminar and in-house training service to help other recruiters improve their sales skills.

To establish credibility within the executive search community, I wrote and self-published a couple of business how-to books entitled *Billing Power!* and *The Recruiter's Almanac*, which I marketed by way of direct mail. In order to facilitate book sales, I set up a toll-free number, and worked out an agreement with American Express, VISA and MasterCard to handle telephone credit card orders.

To my delight, the books sold several thousand copies in the U.S. and seven foreign countries. So, encouraged by my success (and my love for writing), I sold a third book (*Take This Job and Leave It*) and then a fourth manuscript (which you are now reading) to an established publisher.

The point is, my career represents a composite of different activities from which varying streams of income are derived. Sure, it takes a lot of work to juggle so many responsibilities, but then again, my life is never dull or predictable.

Ironically, the biggest problem I have is trying to explain my "job" to the people that I meet at cocktail parties. Am I a head-hunter? A sales trainer? An author? A publisher? Or a direct-mail merchandiser?

## The answer is obvious

I named my company Radin Associates because there are five different partners (each named Bill Radin) running five separate business units.

Does that mean that you should quit your job and start a multi-dimensional enterprise like mine? Of course not. But it does show that it's feasible to parlay your own personality, interests and talents into a livelihood that's rewarding, challenging and consistent with your life priorities, so long as you can deliver a product or service another person is willing to pay for.

The purpose of *Breakaway Careers* is to open you up to the world of possibilities outside the traditional employment market, and to provide you with the tools to carve out an alternative livelihood.

By mastering the ability to function in an independent and self-sufficient manner, you'll join the millions of others who have freed themselves from the constraints, tensions and (yes) insecurities that define the traditional employer/employee relationship. Whether you're motivated by inspiration or circumstance, you can achieve professional satisfaction, financial security and personal fulfillment—and do it on your own terms.

## A universe of choices

The sheer number and variety of breakaway career opportunities is staggering. If you were to add to the government's published list of more than 14,000 occupational titles all the entrepreneurial, unconventional and hybridized careers, you could fill a filing cabinet the size of Rhode Island with no problem at all.

Since many breakaway careers tend to defy classification and because there are simply too many specific options to list, I won't try to pigeonhole you into a specific niche. For the most part, your own set of interests, talents and personal circumstances will largely shape your career anyway. Besides, new opportunities tend to spring up overnight. And with a little creativity, it's very possible that you'll be able to launch a totally unique venture, one that no one else has thought of or can ever hope to duplicate.

Perhaps you'll start up a mobile knife-sharpening service or do fashion consulting over the phone. Or maybe you'll buy a bathtub refinishing franchise, or invent an organic spray-on hair replacement product made from the cloves of imported elephant garlic. The possibilities are limited only by your own imagination and desire to succeed.

## What to tell the naysayers

Unlike niche-market books dedicated to a specific opportunity or type of industry, *Breakaway Careers* is designed to help you choose with an open mind the path that's right for you. Therefore, the different vehicles for a successful breakaway career will be laid out thoroughly and objectively. That way, you can examine your options carefully before you take action or get locked into a financial commitment.

My goal is to facilitate your efforts by giving you the means to identify and research the career of your choice, and to share with you hundreds of proven tactics you can use right away to initiate and *maintain* a nontraditional livelihood.

Throughout the process, I also plan to infuse you with as much encouragement as I can, not only because I believe in the rewards that come from pursuing a breakaway career, but because I want you to have fun along the way.

Remember, nothing takes the wind out of your sails faster than negative energy; and, believe me, nothing attracts negative energy faster than a new idea or a different approach to life. For sure, you'll encounter plenty of naysayers; but whatever you do, be nice to them. Sooner or later, they'll probably be asking you for advice as they launch their own breakaway careers!

# Chapter 1

# Setting Your Sights
# on the Breakaway Life

If there were a theme song to describe the world of work at the turn of the millennium, it would probably be Duke Ellington's "Things Ain't What They Used To Be."

As a prelude to conceptualizing your breakaway career, it might be helpful to step back a minute and reflect on some of the profound changes that have altered our work relationships over the past few years, and how they'll likely affect your life in the future.

We'll start by examining a fairly typical 40-something named Art. Chances are, you'll feel some affinity with him as you take a look at his life.

## When Ozzie met Harriet

Like most people born in the post-war era, Art grew up in a culture in which Ozzie Nelson worked at the office and Harriet stayed home to raise David and Ricky. Unthreatened from abroad and prosperous from within, America of the 1950s and '60s offered a burgeoning middle class the promise of a college education, a secure job and a comfortable retirement.

That this idyllic societal paradigm would ever shift was as unthinkable as a high-quality television set from Japan or a personal computer on every desk. The sweeping changes that were to forever affect the lives and livelihoods of millions of people loomed too far off on the horizon to be clearly visible. As far as the *Hound Dog* generation was concerned, the engine of full employment was humming away at full throttle, with no end in sight.

As the happy days sped by, many of Art's contemporaries read from their baby-boom life scripts verbatim. College degrees in hand, they sanguinely swelled the ever-increasing ranks of doctors, lawyers, teachers, engineers, accountants and administrators needed for the care and feeding of the ravenous and ever-expending economic beast. Hitching up to the American dream, the newly enlisted employees of corporate America rode their careers with silent satisfaction into a predictable world of 30-year mortgages, disposable diapers and 401ks.

## The road less traveled

Art ventured down a different path. Inspired by the heightened climate of creativity and idealism of the late 1960s, Art threw caution to the wind and pursued a fairly unique calling—as a freelance musician. After dropping out of a big Midwestern university, Art plugged his electric guitar into every nightclub, theater, movie set and cruise ship gig he could rustle up.

Admittedly, it was a fun life. He saw the world, met lots of interesting people and eventually ended up in Los Angeles, where he performed with a myriad of musical creatures, from the lowliest lounge lizards to the loftiest stratospheric stars. For over a decade, Art strummed his way through stage and classroom, where, driven by an academic curiosity, he was able to earn a bachelor's and master's degree in music performance.

## Trading one stereotype for another

Alas, reality eventually reared its ugly head. After all the time Art spent in the business, all he had to show for his musical career was a $20,000 student loan debt and an apartment at *chez*

*Goodwill*. It finally dawned on Art that there was about as much money playing music for a living as there was playing triple-A ball for the Albuquerque Dukes. At 30, he'd broken the five-figure annual income mark only once in his life, and not by very much.

So, faced with certain poverty, the idealist guitar player of the '60s and '70s became the yuppie executive of the '80s.

Of course, it wasn't too difficult to buy into the *greed is good* mentality of 1985 Los Angeles. What with movie stars and BMWs filling up every TV screen and rear-view mirror, a life dedicated to stalking the big bucks seemed pretty nifty. Just play the game, don't worry about the other guy and everything'll be fine. Love ya baby, don't ever change.

## The fast lane to nowhere

With a little bit of hustling, Art got himself a job as an executive recruiter, a move that radically changed his finances, his associations and his perspective on life.

Of course, Art couldn't have cut his corporate teeth in a better place than Southern California. In the *Star Wars* age of executive search, where finding jobs for aerospace engineers was like shooting fish in a barrel, it wasn't long before Art was pulling down a six-figure income.

Art had it all: the upscale office in Century City, the luxury car, the mobile phone, the condo in the Valley, the designer girlfriend—and not much else.

## The writing on the wall

Ultimately, though, the high-pressure world of corporate decorum and conspicuous consumption wasn't for Art. As the '80s came to a close, he had a hunch there was more to life than winning the rat race. Besides, certain cracks were beginning to appear in the economic Tower of Babel.

For the first time in years, Art took a good, hard look at the world around him. He noticed that wages for certain jobs had become grossly inflated. It made no sense, for example, that a college grad with a couple of years of experience should be earning

$45,000 a year designing a satellite tracking system that would never be deployed.

Art also found that many of the jobs in the organizations he served were either redundant or totally lacking in substance. And that a high percentage of executives in key positions were mismanaging their companies and leading them to ruin; or, worse, selling them off to merger-mongers like so many lambs to the slaughter.

In addition, Art observed that environmental regulations and high union wages were beginning to force companies to either shut down or relocate to foreign soil. And that, curiously, the federal government was eagerly going broke as it continued to fund the costliest peacetime military buildup in history.

Finally, he saw that for millions of hardworking people, the pressure to keep up with the ever-rising standard of living was forcing both parents out into the workplace, even though a double-income lifestyle meant a breakup of the family unit.

Even before the country had begun its slide into a deep and dismal recession, Art sensed that the 40-year bedrock of full employment and lifelong job security was about to erode. The American Dream was fast becoming the American *nightmare.*

The handwriting was on the wall, and needless to say, Art didn't like what he was reading.

## The common ground

So Art packed his bags, sold the condo in the Valley and moved to higher ground, where he's been enjoying a breakaway career since the dawn of the 1990s.

Of course, Art's story has a familiar ring to it, because Art is me.

But he may also be you, for two reasons.

First of all, the economic tidal wave that's swept across my career landscape has probably created a watershed of sorts in your life as well. You're either working harder for less money, or you're dealing with some form of job insecurity. Maybe even outright unemployment.

And second, you and I share some very common, yet *powerful* personal characteristics that have helped shape our occupational destinies and may very well hold the key to the future.

16

## Girl Scouts and paper routes

Certainly, you've been an idealist at some point at your life, right? My idealism found its expression in playing music. I loved music and everything about it unconditionally, and I sacrificed a lot in the way of time and creature comforts to pursue my dream of performing for a living.

In your case, the outlet for idealism may be an intense desire to save the rain forests or run for mayor or raise goats in Montana. However it manifests itself, the idealism is there somewhere.

You also have an executive demeanor, whether you know it or not. You faithfully balance your checkbook, or you manage people where you work, or you organize the logistics of your annual church retreat. And, like me, you have a bit of the entrepreneur in you. You sold Girl Scout cookies or had a paper route as a kid. At the very least, you got the best price you could on a used car or took the initiative to refinance your home.

## The change of a lifetime

Well, now's the time to put these underlying talents to work and break free from the bonds of the traditional (or what I call "inert") employment framework.

Sure, the change can be scary. As management trainer Brian Tracy likes to say, nobody minds change if it involves winning the lottery. If change means that everything stays the same only gets better, well, that's not so bad.

But when massive, accelerated change means that your law school education no longer translates into a job offer, or that your middle-management position has suddenly evaporated, or that your pension has been "renegotiated away" after 35 years of loyal service, then there's definitely a problem; a problem so pervasive that self-employed Americans now number over 25 million, with an estimated million more signing up every year.

## Polar bear control

In my opinion, nothing can compare with the feeling that comes from being your own boss. Sure, there are the nifty outward manifestations, like setting your own hours and adhering to your own dress code.

And naturally, as a breakaway, there's no way you can be fired. How's that for job security?

But it's the feeling of *control* that you'll find the most rewarding. In the inert world, how many times can you make decisions independently, exercise your freedom to try new ideas or move your business wherever you want?

You can be successful in whatever endeavor you choose, if you'll simply capitalize on the personal qualities that lie dormant in your psyche: your idealism, your executive demeanor and your entrepreneurial inclinations.

I call these qualities the *big three*, and their presence will help condition you for the changeover from an inert to a breakaway career, similar to the way a member of the Polar Bear Club prepares for the annual Arctic swim by taking a series of cold baths.

## Idealist, executive, entrepreneur

A healthy dose of each of the big three, taken daily like a mental multi-vitamin, will give you the strength to put your new livelihood together and meet the daily demands of business.

For example, it's to your advantage to be an *idealist*, so you can:

- Pioneer your individual enterprise.
- Commit the energy, resources and time it takes to get the results you want.
- Advocate the benefits of your efforts to others in order to enlist their support.
- Give your cause a higher purpose than simply collecting a paycheck.
- Persist in overcoming the inevitable obstacles and discouragements.

Of course, it's not enough just to be an idealist. In order to function smoothly and self-sufficiently, you'll need the skills and inclination to deal with the world as it actually is, not the way

18

you'd like it to be. Otherwise, you may end up like a 20th-century Vincent Van Gogh: independent, forward-looking—and broke.

To avoid the potential pitfalls of unadulterated idealism, you'll need to have a bit of *executive demeanor* to help you:

- Hold your own in the bottom-line world of business.
- Master the organizational skills needed to run a smooth operation.
- Delegate responsibility.
- Measure the accountability of those you depend on.
- Assume responsibility for your decisions.

Unfortunately, executive skills alone won't cut it in a one-man band, especially if you're accustomed to relying on someone else to manage the less glamorous details of daily commercial life or promote you into increasing levels of authority. Ironically, the higher you climb the conventional corporate ladder, the more likely it is that you'll lose sight of the way the "common folk" live. High-powered and well-to-do executives tend to insulate themselves from the rest of society, which is OK in the boardroom but fatal in the basement.

That's why you also need the self-reliance and in-your-face reality check of an *entrepreneur*, so you can:

- Work independently, without the need for external motivation.
- Develop the good judgment to make crucial decisions.
- Keep your eyes open for new opportunities.
- Assume the necessary risks to grow your business.
- Gain the insights that can only come from a life on the front line.
- Learn and continue to grow from making mistakes.

Entrepreneurs are keenly aware that nothing ever gets done by itself (and rarely in the way it was originally intended). "The check's in the mail," "It was working fine when we shipped it," and "You wanted it in blue, didn't you?" are typical of the recurring phrases that give veteran entrepreneurs migraines—as well as a healthy business perspective.

# The breakaway persona

While it's certainly possible to succeed without the big three, consider this: If you lack idealism, how likely is it that you'll stay enthusiastic about your work? (This is all the more reason to select a field you have a passion for.) And without executive skills, what will happen to your business if you can't logically deliver to your customers' specifications, or balance your own checkbook? Or, for that matter, how long will you stay profitable in a competitive world without a bountiful supply of entrepreneurial street smarts?

To measure your strengths as an idealist, see how you respond to the following:

*True False*

_____ _____ I actively participate in community activities.

_____ _____ I solicit support for political office-seekers.

_____ _____ I attend town meetings and fund-raising functions.

_____ _____ I volunteer my time for worthy causes.

_____ _____ I diligently strive to improve my athletic ability or physical fitness.

_____ _____ I channel much of my spare time into hobbies.

_____ _____ I devote a lot of energy to self-improvement.

_____ _____ I try to spend extra time with my family.

_____ _____ I enjoy the creative arts and self-expression.

_____ _____ I go out of my way to help those in need.

_____ _____ *Idealist score*

Community involvement or volunteer work are indicators of idealism. Some of the most successful breakaways I know started out in their traditional careers as social workers or political

20

activists. And believe me, dedication to either a hobby or a sport is a sure-fire symbol of passion—one of the most telltale signs of a winner.

To test your business sensibilities, see how you relate to the next group of statements:

*True False*

_____ _____ I keep a daily checklist of things I need to do.

_____ _____ I pay my creditors on time.

_____ _____ I know my bank teller and postal clerk by their first names.

_____ _____ I balance my checkbook.

_____ _____ I keep my appointments.

_____ _____ I resolve disputes quickly and fairly.

_____ _____ I return my phone calls promptly.

_____ _____ I read the business section of the newspaper.

_____ _____ I refer to an appointment book or calendar several times a day.

_____ _____ I generate effective business communications.

_____ _____ *Executive score*

The ability to execute basic organizational and administrative tasks is a sure sign of an executive mentality. Unless you have the means to function in the adult world, you'll have a lot of trouble establishing credibility, collecting receivables and paying your bills.

Somewhere in between raw idealism and dispassionate executive minutiae is the entrepreneurial verve needed to fuel a breakaway career. See how you score on the last set of assertions:

*True False*

_____ _____ I enjoy meeting new people and sharing ideas.

21

\_\_\_\_ \_\_\_\_     I look for the best possible price on items I purchase.

\_\_\_\_ \_\_\_\_     I prefer to deal with the top dog in any organization.

\_\_\_\_ \_\_\_\_     I get a kick out of making a sale or signing a deal.

\_\_\_\_ \_\_\_\_     I become impatient when minor details bog things down.

\_\_\_\_ \_\_\_\_     I invest money assiduously when I feel there's a potential return.

\_\_\_\_ \_\_\_\_     I study human nature and the things that motivate people.

\_\_\_\_ \_\_\_\_     I recognize that different people have different motivations.

\_\_\_\_ \_\_\_\_     I consider myself as being just as important as the next person.

\_\_\_\_ \_\_\_\_     I like to see the results of my own efforts.

\_\_\_\_ \_\_\_\_     *Entrepreneur score*

How did you score? Obviously, the *true* responses in each category represent the respective mindsets of the idealist, the executive and the entrepreneur. Since it pays to maintain a well-balanced breakaway persona, ask yourself how you might improve on any deficiencies. Or at the very least, see if you can capitalize on your strengths and minimize your weaknesses in whatever career you pursue.

## Wearing your strong suit

Understanding your own personality can help you run your business more efficiently. Rick Oseas of Cincinnati, Ohio, for example, is a breakaway who provides highly technical consulting services to large corporations. Soon after he started his practice in 1991, Rick found that the best way to market his service to prospective clients was through a program of aggressive and continuous telemarketing.

However, this approach presented a problem, since Rick would rather walk barefoot over a 10-foot bed of burning coals than make 50 cold calls every morning. However necessary it might be, the *grind-'em-out* process of repetitive, low-yield telemarketing doesn't appeal to Rick, who'd prefer to spend his time at the computer, performing the actual work.

The solution? Rick struck a deal with several freelance telemarketers (other breakaways, as it turns out) he trained to make the initial sales calls. By subcontracting to others the portion of the business that's not his strong suit, Rick gets to concentrate on what he does best.

## People, things or information

Since no single individual can cover all the bases, the best strategy is to play within your game. Many organizational psychologists believe that each person is born with an occupational tendency toward people, things or information. Before you select a role in which you'll be hopelessly miscast, you'd be wise to examine your preferences. You may save yourself a lot of aggravation down the road.

No doubt you've been sneered at by a waiter or insulted by a telephone operator sometime in your life. Didn't the experience make you wonder why anyone who dislikes people so much would ever go into their line of work?

I knew a woman who got some pretty timely advice from an older and wiser friend. After free-associating about law school as the next step in her life, the woman was told, "I guess law school would be OK for you. The only problem is, once you've finished with law school, you'd have to be a lawyer."

If you're concerned that your personality or disposition may stand in the way of a new livelihood, you can always consult with a career counselor or industrial psychologist. Though their findings may not always be completely accurate (or only reinforce what you already think is true), their professional insights can be pretty valuable, and may help you identify areas of relative strength or weakness.

One of the biggest reasons for breakaway failure has nothing to do with the determination or amount of funding that goes into a given endeavor. The failure is caused by a mismatch between the dominant personality traits of the breakaway and the requirements that go along with the profession.

Creative types who can't sell their services, big-shot executives who can't deal with the nuts and bolts and entrepreneurs who can't handle their finances are more often derailed by their lack of strategy than their lack of sweat. That's why psychology is such an important part of success, and why your personality will often determine your options.

Spend the time it takes to learn who you are; it'll be one of the best investments you make.

---

*The foundation of your success will be the love for what you do.*

# Chapter 2

◆

# Embracing a Success Mentality

◆

An "employee" mentality and a breakaway mentality are two different things. Whereas in your former life many of the daily intrusions and distractions (from business insurance to collections to copier maintenance) were deflected by someone else, in your new life you'll be bombarded on a fairly regular basis by fragments of new information, each screaming for your immediate attention.

Much like running after a train that's just pulling out of the station, the less baggage you take with you, the faster you'll leap aboard. To lighten your load, leave behind any negative feelings or unresolved issues you may have toward your boss, your office or your former company. The last thing you want to do is stay chained to the past. I know several people who've either wasted valuable time by fretting over a few unsettled debts or lost sleep by worrying about a performance critique at an exit interview.

Starting a new business takes a whole lot of concentration. So the less you devote to what *was*, the more you'll be able to apportion to what *will be*.

## Warming up to the task

Even with the most meticulous planning, it's normal to feel overwhelmed at first by the minutiae of commerce, both in the startup phase, and after your business is established. At times, building a breakaway career can resemble building a house. That is, no matter how wonderful the blueprint is, once construction begins you'll most likely be faced with redesigns, additions, cost overruns and delays. This can be aggravating to say the least, especially when you've fixed certain deadlines for yourself, or made delivery promises to others.

The best approach to setting a reasonable timetable is to accept the fact that your business, like Rome, won't be built in a day. (If you're a type-A personality like me, this concept will be especially difficult to accept.) Allow yourself the time to do things right, and build into your ramp-up phase sufficient leeway to make decisions carefully before you act. Frequent changes in plans will be counterproductive, so be sure to warm up to the various tasks before you pull an entrepreneurial muscle.

## Moving a stationery object

Let me tell you about a big business boo-boo that cost me dearly in terms of money and aggravation. I was so certain that I was going to move into a new house (which was also to be my business space), that I ordered a large quantity of stationery in advance of the relocation.

I applauded myself in advance for being so clever and *proactive* by having my letterhead, envelopes, business cards, address labels, memo pads and rubber stamps made, so they'd be ready the day I moved in.

The only problem was, my wife and I decided at the last minute to buy a different house on the other side of town. So not only was I stuck with about $400 worth of useless stationery and supplies, I had to go through the whole printing routine all over again. By waiting until I'd actually moved in, I would've been a lot better off (although I'm sure the printer didn't mind getting another big order).

If there's any silver lining in this cloud, it's the fact that I postponed a marketing plan of sending 1,000 form letters to all my clients announcing a new address—to which I never moved—and a phone number that was never connected. Luckily, I avoided a credibility disaster (and logistical nightmare) of major proportions.

# Initiation into the breakaway club

It's safe to say that all careers have some aspects that are difficult to deal with at the beginning. And breakaway careers are no exception. As you begin to embrace a totally new lifestyle and self-concept, you'll undoubtedly experience all sorts of feelings, some of them new and not so pleasant.

This is only natural, since major life changes are generally accompanied by a heightened level of stress. However, if you and those who care about you know what to expect from the changes that await, you can prepare yourself for the initiation into the breakaway club.

Of course, you can't join an exclusive club for free; there are going to be *initiation fees* to pay, so to speak, such as:

- *Fear of the unknown.* Working for a company is one thing. *Being* the company is something else. If you can embrace Murphy's Law like an on old friend, you'll be less surprised by the unexpected. That way, you can let the disappointments or setbacks roll off your back.

- *Increased hours.* When the stakes are high and you really care about something, the tendency is to do whatever it takes to be successful. Even confirmed workaholics are surprised by the sheer amount of time and effort it takes to run a business, and how often the "just-one-more-thing" syndrome will lure you into burning the midnight oil.

- *Roadblock frustration.* Inevitably, you'll have to deal with a government agency, law firm, accountant, certification board, inspector, partner or whatever wittingly or unwittingly impedes your progress or makes life miserable. Sometimes, even the best-laid plans of men and women can sometimes get chewed up by rats.

- *Financial hardships and income peaks and valleys.* Aside from the possible cash investment you might need in order to get things rolling, you'll be faced with a great deal of uncertainty during the time it takes to ramp your business up. As you work toward your goal of reliable (and healthy) paychecks, you may have to live by your wits and make certain adjustments in the way you plan your purchases or prioritize your expenditures.

You may find, for example, that the extended vacations, fine dining experiences and new clothes you gave little thought to affording in your past life may have to be put on the back burner for a while. I'm not suggesting your standard of living will automatically go into a free fall from a caviar to a tunafish lifestyle; but it may be necessary to delay your need for gratification in order to get your business off the ground.

## Your monthly dues

Initiation fees are only a part of your ongoing membership in the Breakaway Club. Here are some more goodies that make up your monthly dues:

- *Additional or unexpected responsibilities.* As a one-man band, you'll need to learn to play all the instruments; or at the very least, know how to conduct the other players. For example, I never really *wanted* to learn how to sort, color-code and bundle 5,000 pieces of bulk mail—but it was something no one else was going to do for me. Once I understood the process, it was easy to hire and train part-timers to help out.

- *Unrealistic or unfulfilled expectations.* I've heard many breakaways tell me with absolute certainty that their businesses would be in the black after only one year. The problem is, there's no way to accurately predict customer trends or cash availability, even in the best of times. Rather than build yourself up for a letdown, give yourself reasonable goals to achieve. That way, you can take pride in your accomplishments, rather than beat yourself up for your shortcomings.

- *Exaggerated feelings of disappointment.* If you're like most breakaways, you're self-directed by nature and tend to be your own toughest critic. Don't expect overnight success.

If you need to get rich quick, buy a bunch of lottery tickets or marry a millionaire.

- *Peer pressure.* Wouldn't life be simple if you didn't care what your friends thought? Unfortunately, it's human nature to seek approval, which won't come easily from peers who may not understand or relate to your nontraditional situation.

- *Competition anxiety.* You and Fred went into the same retail business exactly a year ago and he can't keep customers away, while you struggle month to month to pay the rent. While it's natural to measure yourself against the competition or your business peers, you need to focus on *your* progress, not worry about the other guy.

- *Social realignment.* With evolving interests and recalibrated priorities, you may find that you and your friends from the old job have less and less in common. But take heart; you'll quickly develop new acquaintances and social relationships as your associations begin to change.

Paying dues is a natural part of the breakaway process. After all, you don't get something for nothing. Try to look at the emotional and financial investment you're about to make as something that will enrich your life and benefit your family for years to come.

## Diffusing the family feuds

One of the most delicate issues you may face as a breakaway is the impact your decision will have on your family, especially if they're mentally rooted in the "job security" mirage that you and I know to be quickly evaporating.

To the uninitiated, a breakaway career may appear to be fraught with risk or even foolishness, and it's understandable that to a spouse or dependent, the realization that you're about to eschew a conventional livelihood might seem unnerving.

The best way to reassure loved ones who may feel threatened is to let them know that your decision is sound and carefully considered; and that your new career goals are compatible with their interests.

Full employment, you should explain, is a vestige of the past, and that the very reason you're launching a breakaway career is to ensure the well-being of yourself and those who depend on you.

You might also point out that happiness and excitement have a positive impact on a relationship, and that occupational satisfaction is an important element in life. After all, what would the world be like if everyone's work were simply an obligation, rather than the means to personal fulfillment?

When discussing your decision to pursue a breakaway career, you should let your family know that a new career involves a long-term commitment, and that everyone should fasten their seat belts for a potentially bumpy ride ahead. The last thing you need is the distraction and *angst* that come from someone you love laying a guilt trip on you or expecting overnight success.

If you ever hear something like, "It's been three weeks and you still haven't landed a big account!" or, "When are you going to quit consulting and get a real job?" simply reply, "We're right on schedule. Before you know it, we'll be better off than we ever were."

## The tradeoff factor

Each of us has a particular threshold when it comes to making tradeoffs, whether they're related to finances, work environment or lifestyle.

Joe, for example, is a successful franchise owner I know who's incapable of working past 5 p.m. or on weekends. He became conditioned during the years he spent as an executive with a major chemical company to leave his job at the office—a discipline that he's carried over into his breakaway career.

Vic, on the other hand, has become increasingly obsessed with his career over the years. Also a highly successful breakaway, Vic not only operates his business from home, but interrupts his work only when he's fast asleep, which is an average of four hours a night.

At some point, you'll strike a balance between the hard work you need to run your business and the lifestyle goals you expect from your new occupation. Some people can power through life at full throttle, while others need to pace themselves lest they suffer from illness or burnout.

# Seeking the balanced life

Real estate expert Mike Ferry has often described his nomadic life as a public speaker as both unglamorous and exhausting. "You think you want my job?" he once kidded an aspiring speaker. "OK. You can do Seattle next Thursday, Orlando on Friday and Pasadena on Saturday."

Although he spends the major portion of his life in hotels, airports and banquet halls, Mike feels the tradeoff is worth it.

Does he have a balanced life? "Truthfully, I don't even know what that means," said Mike. "All I know is that what I do works for me. I make a great living and I keep my family happy."

Since your income is going to be dependent to a large extent on your own personal investment of time and psychic energy, one of the first and most important questions you should answer is: Can I balance my life in such a way as to enjoy myself? Or will I allow the pressure to push me to the point of diminishing returns?

Of course, only you can design a life that satisfies your needs and keeps your priorities in balance. But the mere fact that you're about to do something for your own benefit will most certainly auger well for your future enjoyment. Remember the old saying:

*It's easier to work 80 hours a week*
*for yourself than 40 hours a week*
*for someone else.*

## Chapter 3

———◆———

# Establishing Your Career Dimensions

———◆———

Once you've taken stock of your professional preferences and emotional resources, you can begin to consider the quality and character of your breakaway career.

Generally speaking, there are three different kinds of career styles outside the mainstream job market. Each style has a certain shape or *dimension* that will fit your needs, but only if your needs are carefully measured, much the way a tailor might measure you before crafting a flattering new suit of clothes.

The unique features of your career aspirations are of utmost importance, and must be taken into consideration before you invest in a custom-order venture. Without taking the proper measurements, your time and efforts may very well be wasted from designing a professional life that doesn't match your dimensions.

Common sense will tell you that there's a world of difference between, say, writing a book and opening a restaurant. But aside from the obvious dissimilarities in terms of investment capital, licensing laws, lifestyle and so forth, what is it exactly that differentiates the two types of work?

# The personal density factor

Simply put, the degree to which your direct involvement is necessary to execute your chosen work effectively and profitably is what determines your career dimensions. I call this involvement your *personal density*, of which there are three levels: high, medium and low.

A *high-density* career is one that says:

> "I am the *only person* who can do this job.
> Without my physical presence or direct involvement,
> there can be no income earned."

Actors and musicians, for example, know that if they're unable to perform, they're out of a paycheck. The same is true for direct sales professionals, writers, public speakers, athletes, consultants, and so forth.

As a high-density breakaway, I've been excused from jury duty for over 10 years. The reason? Much as I'd like to, if I took time off from work to sit in a courtroom, my business would suffer, and my earnings would be in jeopardy. (Unfortunately, the $5 or $10 a day *per diem* given to jurors won't sufficiently compensate me for lost income.)

Though the time considerations may vary from one profession to the next, high-density occupations are all characterized by a one-to-one relationship between the performance of the work and the resulting paycheck. That means that a freelance saxophone player with a 9 p.m. downbeat and a freelance reporter with a 9 p.m. deadline both need to deliver their services before being paid, even though the physical presence of the sax player is required, while the faxed-in story of the reporter will satisfy the editor.

# Signature careers

High-density careers attract the thinkers, persuaders and in-person providers who've chosen to run their professional lives as lone eagles. And high-density careers are tailor-made for unique, highly individualized or even eccentric people whose need for self-expression is tied to their *raison d'être*.

The ultimate in high-density achievement is the *signature career*, in which an individual's persona or creations are closely tied to his or her name recognition. Author Tom Clancy, a former State Farm insurance agent, is just one of the many breakaways to have achieved fame and fortune because of the special qualities of their work. In effect, they've signed their names across our culture or collective consciousness.

By contrast, a *medium-density* career is one that says:

"I am part of a *team* that does the work.
Even though my presence is important,
there will still be a business
without my continuous involvement."

Partners in medical clinics and small service organizations like travel agencies or catering outfits know that though their businesses might suffer from a prolonged absence, the ebb and flow of commercial life will manage to go on without them.

Medium-density careers tend to attract those who either need the camaraderie of others, or have chosen ventures requiring more than one person or personality type to do the work. Partners Tom Bunnell and Dan Hoard, for example, typify medium-density careerists. As the inventors of the *mambo sok* line of casual headgear, Tom and Dan found that they could run a highly effective specialty clothing business better as a team than as individuals, since one of them was the creative type, while the other had a head for business.

A *low-density* career goes one step further in its emphasis on the organization when it says:

"I am the *coordinator* or *supervisor* of the work.
Without me, there may be negative long-term implications,
but essentially my business is self-sustaining."

Owners of restaurants, distribution facilities, machine shops and retail outlets know they can eventually rely on managers or subordinates to handle the day-to-day operations.

Low-density enterprises fit the bill perfectly for people with managerial skills or organizational preferences. People with previous experience in tightly controlled hierarchical formats, such as large corporations for example, often relish the opportunity to rule a fiefdom of their own.

This study of personal density begs the question: Which of these career styles is capable of generating the most personal income?

## Individual avenues to wealth

The answer? All of them. But only in the last few years has the occupational pendulum begun to swing in favor of the little guy.

A generation ago, it was highly unusual for an individual to become wealthy as a high-density breakaway. Without the financial or human resources of a large corporation as a piggyback to fortune, the lone entrepreneur simply lacked sufficient capital to either buy a factory or administer a hive of worker bees.

In the modern world of media dominance and information technology, however, the playing field has leveled out considerably. As in politics, it's now possible to appeal directly to the voters (or consumers) in order to sell your ideas, images or products, and bypass the king-makers altogether, be they political or industrial organizations.

For every Lee Iacocca or John Sculley, there's an equally wealthy Rush Limbaugh or Madonna. The fact is, you'll find more potential for creating a financially and personally rewarding career outside the corporation now than at any time in recent history.

To illustrate the rise of individual wealth potential, consider Mohammed Ali, the greatest and most popular prizefighter of his time. In 1964, Ali, the former Olympic gold medalist who could float like a butterfly and sting like a bee, earned in excess of $100,000 for his capture of the world heavyweight crown. A princely sum, indeed.

But compare that figure with the astronomical $5 million purse earned in 1990 by Evander Holyfield (who was neither a household name nor a legendary talent) for his heavyweight title bout with Buster Douglas. Such extravagant earnings, even for second- or third-rate boxers, are fairly commonplace today, and illustrate the growth in earning power of the individual relative to the company man.

# The work of a hundred others

The fact that the individual can now go toe-to-toe in the pursuit of wealth with the corporate executive flies totally in the face of the old-style career ethic of the industrial age. Less than a century ago, it was Henry Ford who said that he'd rather have 1 percent of the income generated from the work of 100 others than 100 percent of the income generated from his own efforts.

This approach to wealth creation made perfect sense in the assembly-line era of cheap, interchangeable and exploitable labor. To a Ford, Rockefeller or Carnegie, there was no reason why the 100 others couldn't grow to be 1,000 others or even 10,000 others, as long as there was a market to penetrate and money to be made.

Today, it doesn't take the cash engine of an auto assembly plant, an oil cartel or a railroad monopoly to generate wealth. If your concept of "going into business" conjures up the vision of running a factory with 1,000 employees, that's fine, as long as you're prepared to swim against the current economic tide and cough up the dough for labor, capital equipment, insurance, regulatory compliance, taxes, overhead and legal fees.

The information and communications explosion has, in effect, spawned an age of individual achievement, and created a viable (and increasingly attractive) alternative to the good ol' boy corporate ascension script of yesteryear.

In fact, a recent issue of *Inc.* magazine compared the corporate versus the entrepreneurial avenues to wealth over the last 30 years, and came to the conclusion that the young movers and shakers of the world would be best-served to go it alone, rather than join the ranks of Procter & Gamble, General Motors and IBM. In economic terms, the *organization man* is no longer the undisputed king of the hill.

# Income substitution and density fluctuations

Not everyone, of course, is hell-bent on becoming rich. Many breakaways, like myself, are motivated more by lifestyle preferences and the positive feelings that come from autonomy than by the obsession to own beach-front property in Monte Carlo. If riches come, fine; but in the meantime, self-employment represents the perfect vehicle for *income substitution,* the act of replacing that which would be earned as an employee with that which can be earned alone.

With independence comes flexibility. Just because you start out at one level of density, it doesn't mean you're stuck there forever. People often change their business relationships to accommodate fluctuations in their personal and professional priorities.

For example, let's suppose you quit your job as a CPA with a public accounting firm and pursue your lifelong dream to become a magician.

At first, your income is solely dependent on your ability to perform, even though you get help from other people, in the form of advertising, props, costumes, and so on.

As your skill and bookings develop, you begin to make a reasonably good living. But after two years of high-density work, you get tired of pulling the same old rabbit out of your hat 30 times a week. So you join forces with a couple of other *prestidigitators* in your home town and incorporate the Houdini School of Magic, an accredited course of study for aspiring magicians.

The Houdini School represents the transition from a high-density to a medium-density occupation. In your new role, you're one of three partners, each of whom receives a percentage of the overall revenue that's generated. (And you also share in the risk from starting the business.)

Although your physical presence as a teacher and administrator is required on a fairly regular basis by the school, you can take a few days off now and then (without significantly affecting your income), and let the partners take up the slack. Basically, the school operates whether you're there or not.

Because the school is such a success, you and your partners decide that other cities across the country are ripe for a Houdini franchise. So you sell the rights to set up schools in Atlanta, Houston and Philadelphia to new investors. Bingo! Suddenly you've got a low-density career going. Now you're in a position to take an occasional three-week Caribbean cruise, since each franchise location generates income for you, and your physical presence is no longer necessary.

# The level of success

Clearly, there are advantages and disadvantages to each level of personal density. What's important with each is to know what you're getting into, both long-term and short-term. To determine your density inclinations, ask yourself these questions before you launch your career:

### *High-density considerations:*

- If I break my leg, will I still make a living?
- Can I pass my venture on to others or will it wither and die if and when I lose interest, start another business or retire?
- In my particular specialty, am I limiting my income potential by working alone?
- Do I need others around me to keep me psyched about my work?
- Do I have what it takes to be a success on my own?

### *Medium-density considerations:*

- Do I share the same values and goals as my partners?
- Will close interpersonal relationships affect my judgment?
- Will the inevitable differences of opinion negatively affect my stress level or quality of life?
- Can the business survive a split in the core group, or a new addition to the partnership?
- Will a joint venture bring out the best qualities in each partner?

### *Low-density considerations:*

- Am I comfortable with the lack of control that results from relying on other people to generate revenue?
- Do I have the temperament to hire and fire?
- Can I handle the increased responsibility of having a big operation with a payroll, inventory, office space, and so forth?

- Do I want to live a life of higher stakes, where each decision has the potential to affect another person's livelihood?

Since there's no single (or simple) formula for breakaway success, a periodic examination of your preferences will help guide your density selection. Just remember that the path you take should honestly reflect your priorities and professional strengths.

Ron Fry, for example, the self-published author of the *How to Study* series of books, grew his one-man business into a medium-sized publishing firm with more than a dozen full-time and freelance employees. By contrast, Dan Poynter, the wildly successful self-published author of *The Self-Publishing Manual*, happily maintains a solo operation.

Although Ron and Dan, at one point, had careers of identical density and scope, their personal and professional preferences ultimately led them in different directions. By definition, their breakaway careers allowed them to characterize their businesses in terms of the personal responsibility and depth of contribution each felt was appropriate.

## The density connection

It's not uncommon for the type of work you do or industry you associate with to determine your personal density, at least in the beginning.

For example, if you're a software engineer and you decide to hang out a shingle as a freelance programmer, then it's practically a given that you'll be locked into a high-density situation. In other words, your income will be directly linked to the amount of hours you spend behind your clients' CRTs.

However, just because the computer world is your beck and call, it doesn't mean you have to be a permanent fixture at the job site in order to build a career or sustain a livelihood. Your particular expertise (and your interest in sharing it with others), for example, may give birth to the publication of a specialized newsletter in which you do the writing; while the editing, design, marketing, printing, advertising and fulfillment responsibilities are delegated to others. Your contribution as a medium-density publisher is important, but the newsletter won't fold if you catch the flu and stay home in bed for a few days.

Once your publication reaches a healthy (and profitable) circulation plateau, you may choose to quit working on the newsletter altogether, or simply maintain your ownership and continue to receive passive income from its sales and renewals. Or, if the publishing bug bites, you can purchase another newsletter for video game enthusiasts or perhaps start an annual directory of Dallas-based AS/400 programmers and receive a regular income from these publications.

The point is, there's no reason your personal density levels can't rise and fall depending upon how you wish to structure your business; or why a certain industry, specialization or degree of personal involvement will automatically generate more income than another.

You may even choose to structure your business as a composite of different activities, each with its own density level, much like a financial planner might put together a diversified portfolio for an investor.

By carefully considering the density requirements of the career you're about to choose, you'll have a better understanding of what will make you happy and what might eventually become a burden.

*The first step to breakaway success*
*is selecting a career dimension*
*that fits your personality!*

# Chapter 4

# Boot Camp for Breakaways

Whether you hold a vice president's title with your favorite Fortune 500 company or carve wooden totem poles to sell in the local flea market, you've got a career. And the common ground in all careers is that one role or position will inevitably lead to another, or at the very least, provide you with the accumulated knowledge to pursue your next venture.

A key element in breakaway success is the ability to capitalize on what you already do well. Suzanne, for example, is a friend of mine who runs an interesting business. She designs and paints children's bedroom murals depicting fanciful, bigger-than-life cartoon characters of her own creation.

Before she broke away to start Magic Murals, Inc., Suzanne worked for a children's magazine as an illustrator. She was able to translate the skills she developed at her old job into the basis of a new career.

Most of us are like Suzanne, in that the practical training we need in order to get started is already under our belt. Everything we've done in the past, either academically, professionally or as a hobby qualifies us in some way or another for a breakaway career.

The closer you stick to what you already know, the better your chances of success. To cast off into unknown waters is fine, but before you let go of the lines completely, look closely at your existing portfolio of skills and interests. You may be surprised at how much you already can do.

## The verbatim career

Many breakaways simply spin off from their previous employers and start businesses that are essentially the same as the ones they left. (If doing this sounds good to you, remember that your success has a lot to do with the degree to which you love the field you're in.) The principal difference is that there's no boss to inhibit your progress (or to blame for everything that goes wrong).

Running a one-person accounting firm involves the same set of skills as being an employee of a large firm—when it comes to accounting, that is. Where most breakaways have difficulty is in the operations side of the business: the marketing, planning, overhead, and so on. These issues will be dealt with in later chapters, and can present major problems if not fully understood.

However, the natural advantage of spinning off into a verbatim career is that the skill portion of the business is largely taken care of. To paraphrase the old saying, why reinvent the wheel if you're already on a roll?

## Learning to sail alone

When I spun off from a large executive search firm, I was well-equipped to function as a recruiter. However, designing stationery, setting up a corporation, specifying computer hardware and software and working without supervision were another thing entirely. Fortunately, I had the requisite skills to do my job, so I could earn a living while coming up to speed in areas less familiar.

If you're currently employed, think of what you already can do, and especially what might be available to you in terms of training and skill development after you're gone. For example, do you have access to operational handbooks that might teach you more about how the company you work for is run? Are there ways you can cross-train in order to become more fluent in different aspects of your field? Mastering additional skills will not only help you on your current job and keep you focused, but will provide you with a bag of tricks you can take with you when you leave.

Or perhaps you're working as a temp. Is it possible to get an assignment that will expose you to new techniques you might use later on in a breakaway career?

Temp agencies will often work with you to enhance your data processing skills in order to make you more valuable in the workplace (and enable *them* to increase their earnings in the process). If you think learning Lotus or Windows might help you in the future (say, as a freelance administrator), then by all means, take advantage of their help.

Breakaways remind me of the story of the Swiss Family Robinson. As survivors of a shipwreck, they salvaged everything they could when they found themselves all alone on a tropical island. If you think like them and use your imagination, you'll probably find everything you need to build a new life in paradise, stowed deep in the hold of your current employer.

If you feel that additional training or experience will give you the edge in your new endeavor, then don't jump ship until you have what you need to survive.

## Bona fide courses of study

Let's suppose, however, that you want to sail into totally foreign waters, for which you lack the requisite passport. Many fields require special training, or can only be entered by obtaining an appropriate diploma or certification. It would be pointless, for example, to try to start a legal practice without a law degree; and dangerous to offer weekend flying lessons without a pilot's license.

Since some courses of study are synonymous with credibility and excellence in their fields, graduates automatically have the means to pursue a given career. For example, the Graduate Jeweler Gemologist diploma offered by the Gemnological Institute of America carries considerable professional weight, as does the Associate of Occupational Studies degree obtainable from two years of study at the Culinary Institute of America (CIA).

43

With a CIA degree under your belt (plus a year or so of on-the-job training at a restaurant), you'll be better positioned to open a French cafe or start a mail-order gourmet sauce company than someone who doesn't know soup from nuts. There may be plenty more things you'll need to learn before you make it big, but rest assured, cooking won't be one of them.

## Unwritten restrictions apply

Other professions have less conventional or even invisible pre-requisites. I know of several large securities traders, for example, who swear to an unwritten rule never to bring anyone into the brokerage business who's under the age of 30.

On the other hand, 30 is probably the upper limit in an acting career in which you've been typecast as an *ingenue* or a rebel without a cause. The truth is that age, athletic ability and physical appearance will always have serious ramifications in certain careers. Even Nolan Ryan couldn't pitch forever.

You owe it to yourself to find out if your past training qualifies you technically or legally for your new venture; or to investigate whether the career that strikes your fancy is open to "outsiders." If it isn't, you may have to look at other, more accessible options.

## The college of breakaway science

Higher education, which has always played a key role in traditional occupational preparation, has recently begun to recognize and respond to the increasing surge of interest in breakaway careers.

Adjusting to the current and future occupational realities, many colleges and universities now offer an alternative curriculum to their standard four-year fare. "Entrepreneurial" programs, designed for students interested in pursuing nontraditional careers, are springing up all over the country, and are legitimized by the special diplomas or outright degrees awarded to their graduates.

Currently, there are at least 100 business schools that offer students some form of entrepreneur-oriented curriculum. Stanford, Harvard, UCLA and the Wharton School of Business are just a few of the big-time institutions catering to the nation's newly re-discovered love affair with the free enterprise system.

## Hunk of the month club

The school of business's Entrepreneur Program at the University of Southern California, for example, has gained a national reputation for helping students make their way outside the realm of corporate America.

One of the several successful ventures spawned under the auspices of USC was the "Looking Good: The Men of USC" calendar, the brainchild of 19-year old sophomore Nick Colachis. Convinced of the L.A. public's desire to salivate year 'round over the beefcake bods of virile Southern California hunks, Nick put together a highly attractive, color-photo pinup calendar featuring his own perfect-tan fraternity brothers and other physically fit USC undergrads.

As it turns out, Nick's intuitions served him well, and the calendar was a huge success. Before long, several other lines were added to the Looking Good line of products, including (of course) "The Women of USC" full-color calendar.

## The bookworm solution

The nearly infinite number of how-to books on the market represent yet another source of useful information. In fact, many successful businesses have begun with the purchase of a paperback book.

A quick glance at the shelves of your local bookstore will reveal a wide range of how-to tomes, dealing with nearly every aspect of self-employment, from the most general (*Work With Passion* by Nancy Anderson) to the most specific (*The Publisher's Direct Mail Handbook* by Nat Bodian).

In some cases, a combination of books will be required if you wish to stimulate your interest and round off your expertise in a particular field. For example, your selection of a career as an image consultant might begin with a reading of *101 Best Businesses to Start* by Sharon Kahn, and unfold as result of the practical advice given by Kim Gordon in her book *Growing Your Home-Based Business*.

Later on, you might want to browse through *Financial Essentials for Small Business Success* by Jeff Slater and Joe Tabet to help you with your bookkeeping and accounting, and then sharpen your ability to capture new upper-end business *à la* Dr. Thomas Stanley by implementing the principles in his book *Selling to the Affluent*.

On the other hand, it's quite possible that nearly everything you ever wanted to know on a particular subject may be contained in a single volume. When I self-published my first two books, I found that Dan Poynter's *The Self-Publishing Manual* was so complete, no other materials were needed.

## Other publications

Magazines and newsletters can also supply you with practical insights into the venture of your choice. The writers I know read *Writer's Digest* regularly to keep abreast of current trends when it comes to the craft and business aspects of professional writing.

To find the publications that might be useful in your research or self-improvement, go to your local library and ask for the *Standard Periodical Directory*. It lists more than 75,000 periodicals by name or by subject, and includes nearly 250 categories ranging from advertising to confectionery to telecommunications to travel.

Or to investigate the specialty newsletters available, spend some time with *Newsletters in Print*, which is a descriptive guide to over 11,000 bulletins, updates and serial publications available in print or on-line.

Without a doubt, there's plenty of bad advice out there, so be careful. Just because the author of a book or a freelance writer tells you that the smart money's in day-care centers for neurotic poodles doesn't necessarily mean it's true.

## How to SCORE a mentor

Since it's a well-known fact that the majority of new jobs are created by small businesses, many government, university and private-sector programs have been set up to assist the entrepreneur. One of my favorites is the Service Corps of Retired Executives, or SCORE, a program connected to the Small Business Administration.

After giving SCORE a description of your business, they'll assign you a "mentor," a retired executive whose career was spent in a type of work similar to yours. A SCORE mentor can give you the benefit of his or her many years of experience, plus a nice supply of good old-fashioned encouragement.

Another popular program available in many communities is the "business incubator." Usually sponsored by a local university or chamber of commerce, an incubator provides commercial space, training, counseling and support group activities for budding business ventures. The goal of incubators is to wean you off their support and into the business mainstream, where presumably, you'll pay back the investment made by the sponsors by creating jobs (and tax revenues) once you're established.

In locations where manufacturing or high technology activity is prevalent, there are often programs to support business startup or technology transfer ventures. For example, the Small Business Development Center (SBDC) in Cincinnati, Ohio, is sponsored by the University of Cincinnati. Working in close cooperation with the Institute of Advanced Manufacturing Sciences, the SBDC's goal is to promote the development of emerging high-tech companies, especially as they relate to innovations in manufacturing. SBDC also provides guidance for those who want to do business with the federal government, and helps cut through the maze of red tape so often encountered by those who try.

## Don't leave home without it

Correspondence courses provide a flexible and convenient way to increase your knowledge in a wide range of areas—from accounting to travel agent training to juvenile fiction writing to gun repair. If you think correspondence courses have lost their lustre in recent years, consider this: At last count, there were more than 5 million Americans pursuing an education of some sort without leaving home.

The advantage of correspondence study is that you can enroll at any time of the year and learn at your own pace. Often, it's less expensive than traditional classroom education, and you can pick and choose among the courses you need, in the order you need them. However, you should be aware that when investing in a course of study that's either lengthy or expensive (more than one year and requiring several thousands of dollars in tuition costs), the completion rate is a scant 5 percent.

Aside from the training provided by franchises and business opportunities (a subject we'll cover in chapter 15), correspondence courses are available in a variety of media, including mail, computer (stand-alone and on-line), video tape and cable TV. *Independent study* (also known as home study) generally refers to courses that are interactive in nature; that is, you can work one-on-one with an expert who designs the course, guides the study and grades the "homework."

Independent study is an excellent way to finish your degree, acquire certification or learn new skills that you can apply toward a new career. For example, there are lots of home study courses for paralegals, home appraisers and VCR repair people, now that these professions are considered to be hot careers for the 1990s. Some trade associations even offer their own training and certification, such as the American Medical Record Association (AMRA), which offers a study program for medical record technicians.

# Before you take the leap

In contrast, *self-study* courses provide no interaction or feedback with an instructor, other than "ongoing support," usually by phone. What you receive is a pre-packaged training system, usually designed to get you started in a business and streamlined to teach you only what you need to know, and nothing more.

To get more information about correspondence courses, you can contact the National Home Study Council. Founded in 1926, the NHSC accredits and acts as a clearing house for more than 500 different mail-order courses, including everything from truck driving to small engine repair to real estate. For no charge, they'll send you an updated *Directory of Accredited Home Study Schools*.

Assuming you need more training in the field of your choice, there are lots of ways to come up to speed. If any of them require a significant investment in time or money, your best bet would be to verify their legitimacy and potential benefit before you take the leap. Fortunately, today's abundance and availability of information acts as a launching pad for new opportunities, and...

*There's never been a better time to learn new skills for a breakaway career.*

# Chapter 5

---◆---

# Creating a Dynamite Business Plan

---◆---

Desiree had a dream.

She would leave her boring job as a communications manager with a big corporation and start a new career in fabric design, a field that had fascinated her ever since childhood.

One day, Desiree's dream came true—in a manner of speaking.

Without any notice, Desiree was laid off by her company. "It must be fate," she thought. "Now I can do what I really want."

Although Desiree had a fine dream, she also had a problem: She had never had the time or inclination to prepare for its realization. Suddenly, she had to come to grips with the fundamental, day-to-day aspects of a totally new professional identity, without much in the way of real preparation. In other words, she didn't know what it actually *meant* to make a living as a full-time fabric designer.

How would she get paid? Who would be her clients? How much would she charge for her service? What sort of materials would she need? How much inventory should she carry? Would she rent space in a warehouse, or could she work out of the neighbors' garage?

# A tangible yardstick of commitment

Desiree was rudely confronted by the nuts-and-bolts issues that form the gap between career fantasy and reality. Her situation put her on equal footing with every person entering the start-up phase of a breakaway career—a situation crying for a business plan.

What is a business plan, exactly? Well, a business plan is like a carefully itemized diagram used by everyone who wishes to start a successful business, no matter what form the business takes.

A business plan acts like a positive self-fulfilling prophesy or affirmation, in that it allows you to visualize in minute detail every aspect of your commercial life before it actually happens. It not only addresses the question, "How do I get there from here?" it also aids in crystallizing the answer to, "Where is it I'm trying to get?"

A business plan serves as a tangible yardstick that can be used on a continual basis to measure your progress and reaffirm your commitment to a well-prepared plan of attack.

And in addition, a comprehensive business plan will help you anticipate and deal with the surprises and pitfalls that are bound to occur in any business venture.

Needless to say, without a business plan, you'll lack the organization and thoroughness to put your ideas to work. The value of a business plan is best told by the old saying, "By failing to plan, you plan to fail."

# Screenplay or surgery?

What does a business plan look like? Is it a monstrous, 30-pound document bound in a three-ring binder like the federal budget, filled with bureaucratic techno-babble and loaded with spreadsheets, pie charts and bar graphs?

Not at all. A business plan can be short and to the point. However, the more detailed your plan is, the more dividends it will yield, as long as the salient points are covered.

A business plan shouldn't be written to impress anyone. Instead, it should be a realistic and honest assessment of the personal, professional and financial assets you bring to the party. And of course, it should also include an equally honest appraisal of your liabilities. Don't mistake a business plan for a Hollywood screenplay. If anything, it should be designed with the same dispassionate objectivity, forethought and attention to detail as a surgical team's pre-op briefing the night before performing a complicated procedure.

## Standing the test of time

To write a dynamite business plan, you need to start with a *mission statement,* followed by a clear set of goals and objectives. Mission statements can range from the modest ("To provide the friendliest, most reliable dry-cleaning service in Denver") to the grandiose (as in General Electric's, "To be the world leader in all key businesses").

The point of a mission statement is to define an overarching purpose for your enterprise's existence, much as a motto might be adopted as an expression of one's guiding principle.

Any group or individual can have a mission statement, such as the familiar *I Shall Return* (Douglas MacArthur) *Semper Fi* ("Always Faithful," the Marines), *E Pluribus Unum* ("Out of Many, One," the United States) or *Commitment to Excellence* ("Let's Beat the Pants Off the Other Guys," the L.A. Raiders).

A powerful mission statement is the glue of consistency that holds your plan together and acts as the foundation upon which the business can be built. Constructing a business without a forceful mission statement that's consistent with your ideals is like erecting a skyscraper in a swamp—it simply won't stand the test of time.

## Goals and objectives

Once your mission statement is clear, you can declare your goals and objectives. These should state exactly what it is you plan to accomplish, and provide a general description of how you plan to proceed.

Let's suppose you want to start a dry-cleaning business. Your goal may be "to cheerfully serve the upscale customers in the

Cherry Grove community of Denver, with the objective of providing meaningful employment to area residents while becoming profitable within the first nine months." Or perhaps you want to be specific about the distinguishing features of the business, as in, "The Goal of Cherry Grove Cleaners is to provide the best and most convenient service to dry-cleaning customers by offering expanded hours, state-of-the-art cleaning technology and drive-up window accessibility in the greater Cherry Grove area."

## Your best estimate of success

After you've explained your mission and your goals and objectives, you need to get into the nitty-gritty of the plan. The structure and syntax are the least of your concerns. Unless you need to show the plan to potential partners or investors and want to impress them with a slick presentation, forget the posterity and focus on the basics.

Your business plan is simply a means to simultaneously design and evaluate the program, warts and all. If what you write ultimately exposes glaring flaws in your approach, all the better. Then you can rework the plan without going broke or causing yourself a great deal of wasted effort or embarrassment.

Some aspects of the plan will necessarily relate to the specific requirements of the business you plan to start. For example, applying for a liquor license may be necessary to open a restaurant, but irrelevant when it comes to software consulting.

Other aspects, such as costs, might be impossible to accurately calculate in advance. You may not be sure, for instance, exactly what your overhead expenses are going to be before you actually start writing checks. However, that's no reason for not writing a plan based on your best estimates. As soon as you begin to see a pattern develop, you'll be better equipped to plan ahead.

## The twenty questions

Several major issues are common to practically every business, and can be addressed in a business plan that answers these 20 questions:

1. *What is the exact nature of my business?* Is it retail, wholesale, business-to-business or service-oriented?

2. *Who are my customers?* What are their demographic and spending profiles?

3. *What are my customers' needs?* Do they coincide with what my business has to offer?

4. *Will I have a sufficient customer base to support my business?* Are there enough people within reach to keep me afloat?

5. *Is my product open- or closed-ended?* In other words, can the customer buy it over and over again (open-ended, like ice cream), or is it a one-shot deal (closed-ended, like retirement property in Arizona)?

6. *Who are my competitors?* Where and how do they operate their businesses? Are they successful? If so, in what ways do they succeed?

7. *What are my competitors doing to serve the same market that I plan to serve?* How do my customers feel about them? Are they so entrenched as to be unbeatable? Or do they have areas of vulnerability?

8. *Why should potential customers buy from me instead of my competitors?* What is my competitive advantage?

9. *How will my business be structured?* Will it be high-, medium- or low-density? Am I prepared to work by myself? If want to work with partners, where will I find them? And if I need to hire employees, where will they come from, and how much will they cost me?

10. *What are my startup expenses?* Can I realistically afford to get into the business at this time?

11. *What will my monthly operating expenses be?* Do I have sufficient capital to pay my bills? If so, for how long?

12. *How will I finance my business?* Will I need to get a loan or arrange some type of equity partnership?

13. *How will I set the prices for my business?* Should I undersell or oversell my competition? Can I charge a fair price in this marketplace and still make a profit?

14. *What do I expect my revenues to be?* Can I set and achieve realistic monthly sales goals? Will cash flow and collection issues be a factor in my business?

15. *How soon will I reach a break-even point?* How long am I prepared to struggle before I show a profit?

16. *What is my ultimate earning potential?* Am I getting into a subsistence business, or one that I can get rich from if I want?

17. *Do I anticipate growth or diversification of the business?* Is this business expandable in its projected format, or can it spawn other businesses, like Wal-Mart spawned Sam's Club?

18. *How will I know if the business isn't working out?* Will I build in a smoke alarm for failure, or will I slowly suffocate without realizing it?

19. *What will I do in case the business falters?* Do I have a reserve of capital or a specific backup plan if market conditions change?

20. *What will I do if the business is a huge success?* Will I have the capacity to handle a large number of orders that come in, or will I have to turn them away?

Finally, you should look deep into the future and ask yourself: Will I always run this business? Or can it be sold, managed by a third party or passed on to someone else when I retire?

If you can answer these questions and incorporate the solutions into your thought process, you're on your way to writing a dynamite business plan.

## A plan, not a prediction

Once you've written your plan, keep it handy and refer to it to keep yourself focused. And by all means, write follow-up plans or supplements on a regular basis.

As your business develops, you'll probably need to make adjustments to your original cost projections or your sales and marketing strategies. If you find that something isn't working, or that new information suggests you alter your approach, then write these changes into a revised edition. Build a learning curve into your plan, and don't push yourself to achieve the impossible. That is, give yourself permission to make mistakes. I can guarantee you that absolute perfection is generally unattainable in business, both in the planning and execution phases.

Remember, we're talking about a plan, not a prediction. If you were clairvoyant, you wouldn't need a plan in the first place.

## A strategy that wears well

Just for kicks, I pulled out the original business plan I wrote back in November 1989, when I first broke away to start my own training company, Innovative Consulting, Inc. If anything, I was conservative with my estimates, and very careful to fully scrutinize the venture I was about to get into (which at the time was fairly unorthodox and largely untested).

Now, four years after putting the plan away, I'm surprised at how well it had worked. I shudder to think of how my business would have turned out had I not written (and followed) such a highly detailed blueprint.

What's amazing in retrospect is that the business plan I wrote either predicted everything that worked in the first year of business or provided me with a backup plan for those things that didn't.

For example, the "Billing Power" business unit generated almost exactly the amount of revenue I had estimated. The plan suggested that I incorporate new programs into my business, which, ironically, resulted in even greater revenues than the original. At the time I came up with my business plan, it never occurred to me to write and self-publish proprietary business books and sell them via direct mail. But sure enough, the original plan allowed for the development of new products, much like a good architectural plan allows for room additions and landscaping.

Most striking of all, though, was the fact that I had a backup plan to shift the focus of the business from training to executive search, in case the strength of the personnel placement industry began to erode (which it did, in early 1991). I can't take credit for prophecy, only good strategic planning. And that's what a dynamite business plan is all about.

*The best thing you can do for your business is to write a dynamite business plan.*

# Chapter 6

---◆---

# Raising the Seed Money You Need

---◆---

*Dear Mom:*

*I trust things are going well for everyone back home on the farm. Please tell Dad I hope his cabbages win first prize at the state fair again this year.*

*As you know, I've been thinking of starting a business now that my city desk job at the "Daily Planet" has been eliminated. Lois (you remember, the reporter friend of mine you met when you visited Metropolis—the one you said looked like she needed a vacation) and I have been doing a lot of research, and we've decided that there's a great deal of potential in this town for a store that sells fashionable athletic clothing and durable, high-quality sporting goods and equipment.*

*If all goes well, Lois and I plan to open our own retail store called "SuperSweats" sometime in the next few months. The only problem is, we're short about $10,000.*

*Any ideas?*

*Your loving son,*
*Clark*

Dear Clark:

We're glad to hear that you and Lois are going into business together. She's such a nice girl. Kind of high-strung, though.

Anyway, I talked it over with your Dad (his cabbages got *second* place this year) and he thought we could probably loan you the $10,000 you need to start your business. You could pay us back over several years, or maybe work it off during the fall harvest.

However, we were thinking that since money is kind of tight here at the Kent farm, you might try a different approach.

You remember Uncle Wilford, the accountant? He suggested you call the Small Business Administration at their toll-free number, 800-U-ASK-SBA. If you qualify for assistance, the SBA, the Department of Defense or other state agencies can make all sorts of grants, contracts and specialized loans to small businesses, but only if you've already been turned down by at least two banks and have at least one-third of the amount you wish to borrow in cash or collateral. The chances of getting funds are slim, since only 20 percent of SBA loans (which have a limit of $150,000) are made to start-up businesses. And these days, most of the money they provide is available only to handicapped individuals or to veterans who served in the military between 1964 and 1975.

Other sources of government money can be obtained in the form of grants from HUD; or from the Economic Development Administration (EDA), which is an arm of the U.S. Department of Commerce. These funds are typically managed by local government agencies, nonprofit development corporations or rural planning districts; and they're awarded to Vietnam vets, people on public assistance, the disabled, women and minorities. (Sorry, Clark, but I have a hunch that your being an alien from the planet Krypton won't qualify you as a minority.)

While we're on the subject of money, Uncle Wilford also suggested you try banks, although they're a lot less willing to lend money these days, ever since those S&L scoundrels caused such a stir a few years back. He says you and Lois may also find yourselves behind the eightball with banks because of the type of business you plan to start—apparel and accessories stores are considered risky by the Loan Pricing Corporation (LPC).

At the very least, bankers will usually give you a hearing, and they'll be happy to critique your business plan. (That, in and of itself, might be useful.) Watch out, though. Uncle Wilford says bankers usually want your proverbial firstborn in return for a loan, so if they lend you money, you can count on putting up that nice one-bedroom condo you bought last year, or even your personal assets as collateral.

Now that I think of it, maybe you could refinance or take out a second mortgage on your condo instead. If you do, you should check with your accountant about the tax advantages or liabilities regarding the interest payments and loans to your business.

We know how badly you want to succeed, son, and we'll do anything we can to help. If necessary, Dad and I will be more than happy to guarantee a loan if the bank thinks we need to. I just thought you might be interested in knowing about all your options before you and Lois take the plunge.

Love,
Mom


*Dear Mom,*

*Thanks for your letter, and for passing along Uncle Wilford's advice. Lois says you're a real angel for offering to loan us the money, but as my business partner, she says we couldn't possibly accept it.*

*She did mention, however, that there are other "angels" out there who might provide us with capital, either in the form of tax-free gifts (pretty unlikely), loans or an investment capital with strings attached.*

*Lois did a story not too long ago about investors called angels who pump money into small businesses like ours in return for equity in the company. It turns out that the annual pool of capital from angels totals in the tens of billions of dollars, with investors usually getting a return much greater than what they might receive from an investment portfolio of blue chip stocks.*

*It turns out that the thousand or so people who invested early in Microsoft, for example, are now millionaires, on paper at least.*

*So Lois and I think we can round up some friends here at the Planet who might be willing to buy into the business. I know there's some risk involved, but with Lois at the controls, what's there to stop us?*

*Your loving son,*
*Clark*

Dearest Clark,

Your father and I were very interested in your angel idea, and thought it had a lot of merit. However, we thought of a few things you might consider before you try to round up money from your friends.

First of all, when you mix business with friendship, you never know what will happen. Remember when Dad's poker buddy Fred swore he could fix Dad's old tractor? It took the two of them nearly two years before they even got back on speaking terms.

Once you get your friends involved in your business (or try to get them to part with their hard-earned cash), you'll open up a can of worms bigger than that old toxic chemical cesspool Fred's family sold to those city-slicker developers.

The point is, you may not want a bunch of nervous nellies looking over your books every Friday afternoon; or worse, selling off so much of your stock that you end up getting voted down each time you or Lois get a new idea.

Uncle Wilford likes the idea of using other people's money—as long as you don't get too personal with the other people. One idea he said you might try is a *private stock offering*. This should only be done after consulting with a good lawyer, since there's all sorts of SEC rules that limit things like exemptions and the number of investors you can sell stock to.

For all I know, you and Lois have a shot at growing a $40 million business in five years that you can take public. If that's the case, then you might be able to interest a *venture capital firm* in backing your start-up, but only if you think SuperSweats will grow at a phenomenal rate (and pay back the investors an equally phenomenal return). Otherwise, you can probably forget about VCs as a source of seed money. Besides, VCs only back about 2,000 start-ups a year, compared to angels, who actually support more than 30,000 businesses.

*Professional venture capital firms* are the big boys, and like to play around with large sums of money pooled from third-party sources, like wealthy individual investors, university endowments, insurance companies and corporate pension funds. They'll probably want to invest $2 million or $3 million at a time, which is far more than you could ever use.

*Venture capital partners*, on the other hand, are successful entrepreneurs themselves, who invest their own money. They'll probably be more willing to help you out with smaller incremental amounts, since they've already been where you're trying to go, and know what it's like to grow a business.

Uncle Wilford says that there's less VC money to go around these days, especially for small, low-tech fish like you and Lois. However, if you have a really solid business plan, you might be able to persuade a venture capitalist to cough up some dough.

Love,
Mom


*Dear Mom,*
*Well, things are looking up for Lois and me.*

*We found a retail space on Main Street for SuperSweats, and guess what? On the second floor of the same building is a health club with an aerobics studio. The owner of the health club (and the building) is a real nice man named Lex, and he's offered to waive our security deposit in exchange for fitness wear for him and his staff.*

*As of yesterday, Lois and I had narrowed down our search for money to three different sources:*

- ***Niche financiers.*** *These are highly specialized organizations with an affinity for high-risk businesses, particularly those that require constant cash flow (like temp agencies), or those whose sales are dependent upon large amounts of inventory (such as retail). In addition to providing working capital, some niche financiers also act in the role of "guarantor" with banks, giving them "insurance" on their loans in the event of business failure.*

- **Consumer finance companies.** *These companies (like Household Finance and the Money Store) specialize in loans to individuals. However, as long as your personal credit history can qualify you, you're free to use the money any way you wish once it's in your hands.*
- **Investment advisor firms.** *These are third-party organizations that find sources of capital for businesses, or in some cases, invest their own money in return for a piece of the action. Usually, they charge a flat percentage of the loan amount at the time the deal is struck.*

*In the end, though, Lois and I have decided to purchase our inventory on credit, using my VISA card and her Optima card. We're very optimistic about our venture, and were heartened by a good omen: Last week, we sold a large order in advance to the "Daily Planet" softball team—25 complete uniforms! With the cash deposit we received, we'll be able to pay our overhead for at least three months. What a relief it is to have a cushion to work with.*

*Mom, I really appreciate your offer for money, but it looks like Lois and I will be able to get our business started on our own. Besides, Dad needs the cash for himself—to invest in a brand-new cabbage crop!*

*Love,*
*Clark*

## Chapter 7

---◆---

# If It's All the Same, What's In a Name?

---◆---

*Rent a Wreck, Airborne Express, Kentucky Fried Chicken, Supercuts.*
Budget Inn, Jazzercise, Rollerblade, Jiffy Lube.
*Lenscrafters, Merry Maids, Circuit City, U-Haul.*

(What do these companies have in common?)

*Merrill Lynch, Smith Barney.*
Dean Witter, Paine Webber.
*Arthur Anderson, Peat Marwick. Price Waterhouse.*

(How about these?)

*Xomox, Xerox, Xycom; ZedX, Zilog, Zoltec, Zonic.*

See the patterns? Each of the companies in the first group have names that tell you what they're all about. Their names act as descriptors of the services they provide, the products they sell, and in some cases, the name provides a bit of advertising for good measure. That is, you'll receive cheerful service from Merry Maids, get a reasonable room rate at Budget Inn and have a good hair day with each visit to Supercuts.

How about the second group? Well, these stockbrokers and public accounting firms each follow an unwritten industry convention of stringing together WASPy-sounding surnames, in the manner of law firms or advertising agencies. I guess we as consumers feel more comfortable and secure knowing that our most intimate financial and legal matters are being handled by pedigreed Anglo-Saxons.

No self-respecting firm in any of these fields would ever name themselves in the self-descriptive manner of the first group. If they did, we might be faced with the choice of investing with Commissions R Us, having our taxes done by Creative Deductions, our legal problems handled by Ambulance Chasers Unlimited, and our buying decisions influenced by Subliminal Commands, Inc.

In the case of Xomox, Xerox, Xycom, et al, there's a sort of high-tech marketing mentality at work. By recycling unwanted syllables into corporate identities, these companies have invented proper nouns that somehow conjure up images of scientific creativity or leading-edge product development. "Something pretty special must be going on at a company named Xycom or Zoltec," the average person is supposed to think.

Of course, the tradition of techno-nomenclature dates back to the early 20th century, when George Eastman, who felt his camera company needed a nifty-sounding name that was easy to pronounce and hard to forget, invented the word *Kodak.*

In recent years, several high-profile organizations have changed their names in an attempt to modernize their image. When Sperry and Burroughs joined forces a few years back, for example, it was decided that *Unisys* had a nice, new-age ring to it. International Harvester, faced with declining sales, figured that a name change would redefine the public's perception of the aging truck manufacturer and give the company a shot in the arm. Hence, the name *Navistar.* And who can blame the Pittsburgh steel company for changing its once-stogy name from US Steel to the more glitzy USX?

## Beyond the birds and bees

The name you give your business will influence its success, in much the same way a book's title will stimulate the buyer's interest. Back in the 1960s, *Beyond the Birds and Bees* became an instant best-seller, although you may be more familiar with the new title the publisher came up with, *Everything You Always Wanted to Know About Sex But Were Afraid to Ask.*

You can name your business in one of three ways:

1. Identify it to your customers according to your product or service (and if possible, illuminate its benefits or distinguishing features, as in the *Shur-Good Biscuit Company*).

2. Characterize it according to the conventions of the industry you're in or the comfort zone of the customers you want to attract (as in Smith, Jones & Brown, Inc.).

3. Distinguish it with a high-tech or invented name designed to create intrigue or the aura of newness, as in NiDex Associates.

Naming your business can be fun and it doesn't cost anything, unless you're convinced you need to hire a high-priced market research firm to test the waters. Against the advice of his publisher, Harvey MacKay titled his first book *Swim With the Sharks Without Being Eaten Alive*; but only after overwhelmingly positive results were reported by a public relations firm commissioned to test-market the title.

## The name is the game

Let's say you're going to open a restaurant. You can either go with a descriptive name like the Tortilla Flats or Chicken on Fire; or baptize it with a conventional name. Lately, a lot of eateries have leaned in the direction of the fictitious Irish innkeeper, which seems to appeal to the fern-bar crowd. (This is the trick used by Hoolihan's, Bennigan's, Flannigan's...you get the idea.)

If you're starting a computer consulting business, you can go descriptive or high-tech, as in Logistic Solutions or Zelitron, Inc. You can get as specific or as ambiguous as you want, as long as the name you choose fits your business or sounds acceptable to your customer base. For example, Macintosh Masters is pretty focused, while Data Systems Services leans towards the generic.

Another common practice in this genre is to piece together parts of your name or the names of your partners, as in Ka-Nor Enterprises (if your name is Katherine North) or Rexmar, Inc. (if you and your partner are John Rex and Jill Martin, respectively).

Or, you can use initials, which have been in vogue ever since IBM, RCA, TRW and 3-M became household names. The market research firm I use is called KLD Marketing, named after its founder, Kathy L. DeWitt. You don't necessarily have to be a high-tech firm to incorporate initials or word fragments into your business moniker—take a look at retail giants such as K-Mart (a spin-off of Kresge) and Wal-Mart.

If you can, try to avoid crossing genres. Otherwise, you may end up with a name like Snappy Computers, which may seem incongruous to potential customers accustomed to a more conservative or high-tech corporate image.

## Names only a mother could love

The old standby, of course, is your own name, plain and simple. Or, if you don't like the sound of your name, use someone else's. I have a friend named Peter Leffkowitz who thought his name might limit his appeal, so he named his clerical staffing agency after his favorite shirt—Pendleton.

Don't worry about being accused of being an egomaniac. In some cases, the name your mother gave you might be the right choice, better than anything fancy or contrived.

However, there are some types of names that are best to avoid. These include names that are:

- *Unpronounceable or overly complicated.* Unless you have a massive advertising budget devoted to untwisting the tongues of your customers, work with the vocabulary that's within the reach of your target market. Avoid foreign names that require fluency in the language (or Anglicize the pronunciation, as in *Chef Boy-Ar-Dee.*)

- *Inappropriate or discordant.* I saw a restaurant named the Tummy Stuffer, and felt a sudden loss of appetite. And I always think of bad breath when I hear the name

Haloid; maybe that's why the company changed it to *Xerox*.

- *Controversial.* True, there are a lot of shysters out there. But naming your garage Honest Ed's might antagonize the other mechanics in your town.

- *Politically or ideologically charged.* Let's suppose you have a company called Born Again Concrete or Right to Choose Liquors. The names may appeal to a certain group of people, but you run the risk of alienating your heathen or pro-life customers.

- *Overused or out of date.* There's no law against naming your tavern the Dew Drop Inn, but by now the play on words is as old as the hills. And for some reason, the word *Zephyr* has lost its lustre; you hardly see it at all anymore.

- *Associated with negative impressions.* Conventional wisdom goes against using the word "Enterprises" in your business name. Somehow, it has amateurish connotations. And the terms "consultants" or "consulting" have also fallen into disfavor, probably since everyone and their brother is now a consultant of some sort, and many people associate "consultant" with "looking for work."

- *Already in use and protected by law.* Hey, I'd probably get lots of business by calling my company the Sony Corporation, but there's a limit to how many customers I could keep with a Leavenworth address.

Do yourself a favor. Pick a couple of backup names just in case the one you want is already taken. Check with the office of your state's secretary of state to find out if the name is already in use, and if it is, whether there's likely to be a conflict.

## Name duplications

Existing names that are specific to a certain product or service are usually protected, especially if the name you have in mind is similar enough so as to cause confusion. For example, Turbowash Car Care sounds enough like Turboscrub Car Wash that the name will more than likely be disallowed. On the other hand, Diamond Jewelry Supply and Diamond Septic Tank Supply sell completely different products (we hope), and therefore, shouldn't be a problem. If you have questions, talk to your attorney.

If you really love the name you've chosen and want to pull out all the stops to use it, you might try the approach I did when I first started my business.

I had selected the name Innovative Consulting, Inc. (which I later realized was a mistake, since it invoked the dreaded *C* word). As it turns out, however, a search conducted by the secretary of state had identified another company that had a similar name, Innovative Resources, Inc.

"Well," said my attorney, "I guess you can't use the name you wanted."

"That's true, " I said, "as long as Innovative Resources is still in business. If, by chance, they've closed up shop, I'm free and clear to use the name."

Later that day, I tracked down the founder of Innovative Resources, and sure enough, she told me the company had folded up several months earlier. The founder was kind enough to write a letter of release to the secretary of state to the effect that she no longer had a use for the name, and I was allowed to incorporate under the name of Innovative Consulting.

## Anteaters and gunslingers

Think of some of the ways a great name can help you get started and fuel your business. The name Aardvark Self-Storage, for example, may be lacking in congruency (what's the connection between insect-slurping mammals and lockable steel sheds?); but you can bet it's the very first yellow pages entry under "Moving and Storage."

Other names can be linked to your business to create an aura of legitimacy, especially if you use world geography as a foundation. The bigger or more well-known the reference point, the bigger the perceived reach of your company.

*Pacific Ventures. Beacon Hill Partners. U.S. Computer Systems. American Community Advertising.* These are names that achieve credibility through association.

Be careful, though, not to overextend your reach. Using the words Global, International or Unlimited might have a deleterious effect, since they appear more pompous than professional.

Adopting a name or slogan that's universally recognized can work in your favor, too, if you're careful to sidestep potential infringement issues and work within the public domain. My accountant's nephew, for example, started a language school in Shanghai called the "John Wayne School of English," which I think is a hoot. His school became an overnight success, largely because of its linkage with the Duke, the most well-known American in China.

Maybe that's why the name association game is so popular—it works. Just ask the founders of Walden Books, Mayflower Moving or Nike footwear.

You can get a lot of mileage out your business' name, especially if it's designed to do the selling for you. And though you need more than just a name to make a living...

———◆———

## *A great name for your business is like money in the bank.*

# Chapter 8

# Cost Containment, Image Control and Legal Self-Protection

*Oh, good morning! Welcome to MegaBucks Industries. We're so pleased to have you on our team as vice president of Central Operations.*

*My name is Ms. Shield, and I'm your personal assistant. I'll be helping you get acquainted with your new surroundings here at MegaBucks. If you have any questions, please feel free to ask.*

*If you'll follow me, I'll show you to your office. Nice desk, isn't it? Go ahead, have a seat.*

*Now, in the left drawer you have all the company marketing materials, sales brochures, direct-mail pieces, invoices and product specifications. Over in the right drawer, here, you'll find company stationery, envelopes, memo pads and rubber stamps, if you need them, along with 500 business cards to get you started. Let me know when you run out, and we'll have more printed.*

*The computer terminal on your desk is all fired up and ready to use. You are familiar with Windows, aren't you? Good. Everything you need can be accessed from the main menu. We have sales figures, contracts, correspondence, regulations, procedures and e-mail.*

*If you need help with anything, just call Brian on extension 115. He's our systems programmer.*

*The Dictaphone is over here. Just let me know what you need typed, and I'll be happy to handle it.*

*Your telephone line is extension 112; fax, 113. Shannon Parr is the receptionist, and she'll route your calls to me, so I can screen them. Is that OK?*

Sure. Because this was just a dream. Wake up; you don't work for MegaBucks Industries anymore, you work for yourself.

# A breakaway, not a dilettante

Money. That's what this dream is about. Money buys the fancy office and the personal assistant and the marketing communications materials and the computer system. Money gets your self-employment venture off the ground, sustains it, and if all goes well, underwrites its expansion. Money buys peace of mind and sets up a nice buffer between you and your creditors, your suppliers and, at times, your family. And money buys protection against the unforeseen, like work interruptions that may result from poor health, natural disasters or the ill intentions of others who prey on small businesses.

Unlimited capital is terrific, but unfortunately it's rarely part of the startup equation, at least for us mortals. If you had great gobs of money to spend to get your business rolling, you wouldn't be a breakaway, you'd be a dilettante.

That being said, it's ironic that the worst thing you can do for your new career is throw a lot of money at it. Oh, sure, if you're investing in Texas oil wells and your father is Prescott Bush, then you can always borrow, say, $300,000, like son George did when he and Barbara were fresh out of college.

But for most of us, money is a scarce and often fleeting commodity, and a cost-containment mentality will prove to be an enormously valuable asset, allowing you to allocate wisely the investment resources you have. As Paul Hawken, owner of the Smith & Hawken Tool Company has pointed out, it's a myth that most small businesses fail because of undercapitalization. In fact, just the opposite is true.

# Capital punishment

Many businesses run into trouble because the owner or owners raise a large chunk of capital, only to squander it unnecessarily. For example, in order to succeed, is it really necessary to:

- Rent office space when you could just as easily operate from your home?
- Purchase new equipment when you could buy it used?
- Outfit your office with electronic gizmos that could either be borrowed or rented (or shunned altogether)?
- Spend a lot of money on customized computer software when a modest investment in off-the-shelf packages (or a trip to the library) would suffice?
- Hire a big-time public relations firm to design your business logo and stationery when you could do it yourself or work with a freelancer?
- Retain an advertising agency to write copy and develop your marketing materials?
- Incorporate your business when a sole proprietorship or partnership would do just as well?

Heartbreaking as it is to see someone go out of business, it's truly tragic when the reason is, "I got into a two-year lease on an upscale office downtown, and the rent killed me," or, "I spent so much money on TV advertising that I didn't have any left over to pay the bills."

There are a lot of valid reasons why a business can fail; but don't let cost-control myopia be one of them. In the beginning, invest in precisely what's vital to your success. Period. Unless the very fabric of your business is tied to outward appearances, resist the temptation to go hog wild with all the frills. Besides, most of your customers won't know the difference or care anyway.

# Heavy metal yuppie

I guess the best example of the irrelevance of outward appearances can be illustrated by Tim Moffitt, a highly successful businessman from Asheville, North Carolina.

Tim is the owner of an executive search firm called Moffitt International. He can make good on the "international" claim because he specializes in the placement of real estate and construction executives in the U.S., Europe and, more recently, Russia.

Tim and I had spoken a few times on the phone, and he eventually hired me to consult with his company. Shortly after arriving in Asheville, I received a call from Tim to arrange a brief meeting in the lobby of my hotel. Based on what I knew from our previous conversations, I had visualized Tim as a polished, Southern gentleman of great sophistication and conservative appearance. After all, Tim was a member of the local Republican Party and had done business with Donald Trump.

But when I wheeled around to greet the man who'd tapped me on the shoulder, I could scarcely believe my eyes. Instead of the squeaky-clean yuppie businessman I'd pictured, there stood a tall, skinny head-banger, dressed like the lead singer of a heavy metal band: boots, black leather jacket, spiked shoulder-length hair—the whole nine yards. *Here, take my wallet; just don't hurt me,* was my first reaction.

"Bill, nice to meet you," said Tim, in a soft Carolina drawl. "I can see the shock on your face, but don't worry. A lot of people react the way you do."

## A man to remember

Well, Tim turned out to be one of the nicest people and one of the most savvy professionals I ever worked with. But one thing puzzled me.

"Tim," I said, near the end of our meeting. "I hope you'll excuse me for asking this."

"Go ahead."

"It's just that, well, your *appearance*. What do your conservative clients in New York and Boston think when they meet you for the first time? Aren't they put off by the way you look?"

"Believe it or not," said Tim, "they just love it. For some reason, all those stuffy East Coast executives get a kick out of dealing with someone who looks so different.

"And one thing's for sure, they certainly remember me, long after we meet."

# Home is where the action is

Now I'm not suggesting you go out of your way to put your customers in shock. I only want to make the point that outward appearances can sometimes be deceiving (or irrelevant), and assumptions about what it takes to succeed can often be incorrect. In Tim's case, he had dispelled the notion that a person has to look just like his clients in order to do business with them. As long as a strong bridge can be built, it doesn't necessarily matter what it's made of.

Another stigma that's rapidly evaporating is the notion that the home is an inappropriate place from which to run a business. In truth, working out of your home is one of the best ways to save money and improve efficiency. Of course, if you're running a retail establishment such as a clothing boutique or a restaurant, or a commercial enterprise where heavy manufacturing is done, then a home-based business won't be practical.

But for nearly every other type of enterprise, the home can be an ideal place to get your business off the ground or even locate it permanently. In fact, the home-based business trend has become so widespread that according to a recent article in the *Washington Post*, there are now more than 41 million households in the United States in which adults are at work, either full- or part-time. This represents an astonishing increase of *64 percent* from only five years earlier. In the town in which I grew up, Alexandria, Virginia, there were more than 1,500 full-time, home-based businesses in 1990, as opposed to only 820 in 1980.

Why the big increase? Here are some of the reasons:

1. *Free rent.* The money you save from the reduced overhead can be applied to other, more important things.

2. *Free transportation to the job.* Why spend money on busses, trains or subways (not to mention parking, gas and auto maintenance) when your own two feet can get you to work?

3. *Reduced commuting time.* Think of the hours you can spend more productively than in transit, sucking up

truck fumes, jockeying for that empty seat or listening to Rush Limbaugh.

4. *Diminished stress and frustration.* At home, nobody ever cuts me off in traffic, or cares whether I'm five minutes late. Besides, if I ever get stressed out at work, I can get hugs from my wife or hold the cat in my lap.

5. *Increased time with those you care about.* Working at home connects you to your family, your friends and your neighbors. And since you're around the house or apartment during the day, you feel more like a participant in your community than a weekend visitor.

The most common apprehension about working at home is that it takes so much more discipline than working in an office with a grouchy boss or an incompetent staff. However, I've found just the opposite to be true. For me, it takes far more discipline to get up an hour earlier and worry about what to wear in the morning and fight traffic than it does to sleep an hour longer, put on a jogging suit and stroll to work from the kitchen.

# A worthwhile tradeoff

The second most common apprehension about working from home is that you'll suffer from a lack of camaraderie. There's no denying that you spend more time alone at home—alone with your thoughts, free from meetings, office infighting, peer complaints and other distractions. Frankly, I feel the quiet of the home to be a worthwhile tradeoff for the hubbub of an office. If I find myself getting lonely at home, I simply call a friend and get together with another breakaway for lunch. And for professional advice or interaction, I've found that it's as close as the nearest telephone.

An often overlooked advantage of working at home is the all the money you save from hidden expenses. Consider the additional costs of working outside the home:

- *Auto insurance.* Most carriers add to your policy (or *red line* you) for commuting to work in the city, especially if there's a higher rate of crime where you work.

- *Equipment duplication.* Many people need to keep a computer at both the home and the office, not to mention a phone, a fax and other peripherals.
- *Meals.* Daily lunches and snacks from the restaurant down the street can become habit forming and add up.
- *Clothes.* I don't know about you, but I never seemed to have enough suits, shirts and ties when I worked in an office.
- *Dry cleaning.* Somebody's got to take care of all those nice clothes. I know I never had the time, what with commuting and late meetings, so I spent $30 or so a month for someone else to take care of it.
- *Childcare and baby-sitting.* It feels reassuring to be around in the afternoon when my 14-year-old step-daughter gets home from school, and it certainly eliminates the need to hire a sitter.

Many of the breakaways I know have turned their garages and attics into offices, especially when they need to be isolated from distractions such as crying babies and barking dogs. Since I have neither, a spare bedroom works just fine.

## Diffusing the home office stigma

What about the public's perception of working from home? Won't your customers think of you as small-time or amateurish if they discover that you work from a bedroom and not a boardroom?

Well, in my opinion, the home office phenomenon has become so pervasive that it's no longer an issue, just like it no longer raises any eyebrows when you ask to be seated in a no-smoking section of a restaurant.

Here's how I diffuse the "home office" stigma. I follow a sort of "don't ask, don't tell" policy when it comes to where I work. I make it seem as though I have an office outside the home, but if anyone asks, I tell them the truth. I'm not ashamed of the fact that I work from home, but on the other hand, I don't feel it's necessary to broadcast it, either. To me, the quality of the work comes first, and where it's performed is irrelevant. If someone has a problem with my working from home, it's probably just as well we don't work together.

But just to be safe, I avoid fueling any stigma that might be associated with a home-based business, especially in an image-conscious industry like executive search. For example, even though I type all my own letters, I put *WGR: rbl* at the bottom of all my correspondence, to make it appear as though the letter was typed by a secretary.

Here's another trick: Instead of a simple "Hello?" I answer the phone, "Hello, this is Bill." To an outsider, it sounds like they've reached me on a direct business line, which in fact they have.

By the way, I keep an unlisted number because I don't want my time wasted by telemarketers and other strangers who tend to drain my energy and waste my time. In my home-based business, I don't solicit walk-in (or call-in) traffic, and with an unlisted number, I can keep it to a minimum.

## The media that takes the message

I've found that only two phone lines are sufficient for my needs: one equipped with call waiting, the other hooked to the fax. If my wife or daughter needs to make a call while I'm on the phone, they use the fax line, which won't take incoming calls (it's set on one fax ring before the fax tone begins its warble); and of course, I have them trained to answer the phone "Hello, this is Ruth," or "Hello, this is Randi" if I'm not around to pick up the phone.

I used to have an answering service to take my calls when I was away from my desk, but I couldn't justify the $60 a month. Besides, the service had a tendency to screw up my messages anyway and mispronounce my name. An answering machine did a more accurate job of recording messages, but I could never remember all the codes needed to replay and fast forward my messages when I traveled, and if there was ever a power failure and the machine got turned off, I lost a lot of calls. Besides, the all-too familiar sound of an answering machine really turns off a lot of business people.

What I settled on was a voice messaging system from the local phone company. At around seven dollars a month, it's cheaper and more reliable than an answering service, and sounds a heck of a lot more professional than a machine. In addition, it'll respond to call waiting after four rings and reroute calls to the messaging center if I can't press the switch hook in time.

In terms of my telephone, I use a Panasonic KX-T2365 that I paid around $50 for. The thing is great. It's got a speakerphone, a redial button, a mute button (great when you have to clear your throat), a hold button and an LCD display that logs the time spent on each call. I also use a Plantronics headset, which is indispensable if you spend as much time as I do on the phone. I don't think I could function without it; at around $200, it's the best investment I ever made. The headset not only allows me to use my hands to take notes or pet the cat when I'm on the phone, it also prevents phone-related injuries such as neck strain and backache.

## To lease or not to lease

Aside from my phone equipment and computer, there isn't anything I own that wasn't first rented on a trial basis or done without.

For example, I leased a fax machine for several months until I could afford to buy one. Leasing allowed me to test whether I really needed a fax, and at the same time, try out a specific product to see if it was any good.

As it turns out, the model I leased was a piece of junk (I can't remember the manufacturer, but the thing was always jamming or failing to send documents). So at least I knew what brand to avoid when I went to a discount office supplier and bought my Brother 200, which is simple, and does the trick.

For over a year, I used the "copy" option on the fax machine to make photocopies, or I went to Kinko's after hours when I needed something reproduced. Eventually, I bought a Sharp Z-52 for around $300, and as far as a personal copier goes, I have no complaints with it.

My first computer was a Macintosh SE that I bought used. Bear in mind that you'll never come close to recovering your dollar investment costs in computer hardware, since the manufacturers lower their prices on a continual basis. What you want to do is buy one that's reliable, reasonably current and gives you no more in the way of features and memory than you need. If you try to get clever when it comes to the ultimate resale value, you'll find yourself fighting a losing battle. The computer I'm using now, a Macintosh IIsi, was state of the art when I bought it a year ago, and obsolete today. I know I'll take a real beating when I sell it, but it's such an integral part of my work that I can justify the loss.

My laser printer, too, was used, and I leased it from a dealer for several months before I made the decision to buy it. For nearly five years now, it's proven to be a workhorse and well worth the investment, even though if I were to buy it today, it would sell for half of what I paid for it then.

The peripherals I bought separately are now available as built-in options in many computers. However, unless you think a fax modem or a CD player will generate income for you, then it might be better to buy or lease a used computer and add on to it according to your needs. Of course, one advantage to leasing is that while you lease, product improvements and price reductions will enable you to purchase more for your money at a later date.

Even the hard data I own was bought used. The *Corporate Technology Directory,* for example, is a four-volume hard-cover guide to high-tech businesses that's published annually. The cost for a new set is around $500; but because I bought last year's edition in *soft cover,* I was able to get the whole set for under $200.

## Beware of the software dog

Software is another expense that can be contained. I must have tried a dozen different software packages (for everything from form letters to day planners to will kits) in the last few years, expecting to save time and maximize productivity from each one. Sadly, I spent more time installing them and having them gum up my hard-drive memory than I did using them. Except for a relational database program designed by a friend of mine, I'm doing fine with just the basics: Microsoft Word for word processing, My Advanced MailList for mailing labels and PageMaker for simple desktop publishing chores. All the other packages were more trouble than they were worth, at least for the business I'm in.

If you're considering investing in new software, ask for a demo disk first that you can try, or find out if there's someone who's currently using the one you want who can answer your questions. On several occasions, I've bought software, only to find out after considerable aggravation and dozens of long-distance calls to customer service that the software wouldn't run on my system. To protect yourself, make sure that you can get a refund if the package isn't right for you.

I wouldn't call myself computer phobic, but I get very anxious when computer problems become the central focus in my life. When the tail starts to wag the dog, I know I'm in trouble.

## Stationery on a shoestring

How important is "corporate image" in your business correspondence? Is it worth a $750 to $3,000 initial investment? For most breakaways, it's foolish to spend a ton of money up front to design a snazzy logo and have elegant stationery printed.

With the use of a computer and a laser printer (yours or a friend's), you can design a logo and stationery yourself and save a bundle of cash. Here's how.

First, let's assume you have several different type styles—fonts—to select from, like Helvetica, Times and Geneva. Pick a font that you don't normally use, and make that the font for your logo, stationery and business card, so that the one you use will contrast with the one on your letterhead. That is, if you like to write letters in Times, then pick a font like Geneva for your stationery. Mainly, the contrast is between the *serif* (ornate) and *sans serif* (non-ornate) style of letters.

Next, experiment with the size and placement of your company name, address and phone number on the page that's to be your stationery. If you can get it exactly where you want it, fine. If not, you can cut and paste it into position on a separate piece of paper after it's been printed out, and use that page as the camera-ready copy you take to the printer. Of course, you can save even more by keeping a template on your computer, and laser printing it along with your correspondence each time you write a letter. This is the trick used by those who send lots of documents via fax modem, but I guess I'm somewhat of a traditionalist, and like to have stationery around.

Use the same type-style format on your envelopes and business cards, adjusting for size. Depending on how fancy you want to get, you can add lines or boxes to give your work a little bit of graphics appeal. A logo might simply be an extra large letter with a drop shadow, or a piece of clip art.

The trick is to keep it simple. Avoid the use of screens (varying shades of gray), since these can become problematic in the reproduction process. You can't be expected to get the same results as a professional; the object here is to produce materials that are functional, yet inexpensive. As your business develops and you have the resources to hire a professional or improve on what you've got, then go ahead. Certainly, my own materials have gone through several iterations in the past few years. Just don't invest in needlessly expensive stationery when the same amount of money could be used for something important, like another two months of telephone service, or replenishing salable inventory.

To conserve on envelopes, here's a trick I use: Go to a print shop and have them make a self-inking rubber stamp with your return address on it. That way, you don't burn up envelopes (the most expensive component of your stationery) on nonessential correspondence.

## Friendly advice from a direct competitor

Naturally, there'll be times when a professional's help will be required when designing image-related materials or advertising. Of course, I had to learn this the hard way.

The first time I ran a display ad, I wrote the copy and designed the art myself. As it turns out, the ad was a dismal failure. The only response I got from a quarter-page ad costing $500 in a publication with a circulation of 28,000 potential buyers was from a direct competitor who saw the ad and felt compelled to call.

"Hey, Bill," he said. "I saw your magazine ad. Did you by any chance write the copy yourself?"

"As a matter of fact I did."

"That's what I thought," my competitor replied. "Let me give you some friendly advice: Next time, let a professional do it."

Which begs the question: Can you get quality results that are reasonably priced? In other words, is there an option somewhere between a Pinto and a Porsche?

When your image needs more than a do-it-yourself job, but a public relations firm or an ad agency is beyond your means, the answer usually lies in the freelance world, where the employees of agencies moonlight in order to make extra cash or exercise their artistic freedom.

By networking within the trade, you can find competent professionals (hopefully, rising stars in their industry) who are more than willing to work with you on a per-project basis. After interviewing them and reviewing their portfolios, you'll be able to determine whether their work is suitable for your needs. If you're unsure as to the quality, ask for a sketch or a mock-up before you go into production. You may lose a little time or money during the trial and error period, but you'll save a considerable amount of cash by going the freelance route, rather than dumping your job on a big, expensive agency.

The next time I ran an ad, I took the advice from my competitor. I was able to track down a copywriter and an illustrator who were employed by a well-known magazine. Both of them agreed to moonlight for me at a reasonable cost and develop an ad that was tailor-made to create a strong impression on potential buyers. As a result, the ad generated an average of $7,000 a month in sales for the next six-month period. Total investment in copy writing and illustration: $450.

## Desktop options

In addition to a logo, stationery and business cards, there are other materials that might serve you well, depending on the type of business you have.

For example, a brochure can come in handy if the product or service you provide needs additional explanation or support. A simple brochure can do an excellent job of selling, too, or give technical information or pricing.

Now that desktop publishing is within the reach of the small businessperson, brochures can be produced cost-effectively, and with great flexibility when it comes to making changes in either the content or the numbers produced, especially if you have a standard format that can be varied to suit your needs.

One supplier that's done a marvelous job of providing ready-to-use communications "shells" is the Paper Direct company in Lyndhurst, New Jersey (dial 1-800-A-PAPERS).

By giving you a selection of attractive, full-color formats on which to laser-print your own copy, Paper Direct can transform a lifeless trifold into an eye-catching brochure or self-mailer. As an added bonus, many of their brochures also come with matching pre-printed shells, including letterhead, envelopes, business cards and postcards. For an incredibly low price, you can upgrade your business image overnight. Paper Direct also supplies high-quality laser-printable certificates, invoices, purchase order forms, calendars, labels and reply forms, in addition to a wide variety of regular and recycled blank paper, available by mail order.

## A valuable and versatile tool

Presentation folders can also be a valuable, versatile tool. These 9-by-12 or 10-by-12 pocket folders come in a variety of colors and paper styles, and may be imprinted with your logo or company name. Many print shops will insist that it's necessary to custom-manufacture the folders from paper stock to your exact specifications.

However, faced with such an expensive proposition, I bought attractive blue linen folders wholesale from a paper supply company instead, and took them to a foil-stamping company, along with my logo. The stamping company made a reusable die of my logo, and presto! For around $200 (which included the one-time set-up charge for making the die, plus the $58 it cost for the plain folders), I got 100 all-purpose presentation folders that can be used for everything from proposals, reports, public relations and press releases to (of course) presentations.

Foil stamping and embossing are relatively inexpensive ways of giving your materials a little pizazz. Call around for quotes; the prices and quality will vary considerably from one supplier to the next.

The revolution in desktop publishing has definitely been a boon to the breakaway. Finally, it's possible to present an appealing and professional image to your customers, and still contain your costs. And for those things that you can't do yourself, there are always freelancers to come to the rescue.

## Corporation, partnership or sole proprietorship?

Many breakaways feel the need to "legitimize" their business enterprises through a legal process known as *incorporation*. All too often, though, the motivation to incorporate is driven more by ego than by sound business judgment.

Incorporating your business can give you many advantages, but it can also be a waste of time and money if there's no good reason to do it. Incorporation allows you to:

- Establish and increase equity (or *stock*) in the business, which can be useful when attracting key employees and/or investors.

- Limit your own liability and protect your personal assets from a lawsuit.

However, the initial process of incorporation can be expensive (a competent attorney will charge between $500 and $750), and running a corporation can be confusing and time-consuming, especially when it comes to tax preparation and payment.

In addition, there are all sorts of state, federal and local regulations that can make doing business as a corporation complicated and in some cases restrictive. Most state laws, for example, prohibit corporations from earning interest on their business checking accounts.

If you're going into business with one or more people, a *partnership* will offer a more simple format by which to do business. Partnerships are unencumbered by much of the red tape that corporations have to deal with, and issues pertaining to who owns what and how the profits are split can be dealt with a lot more simply than in a corporation, where stock ownership represents the final word or *raison d'être*.

For a one-person operation, a *sole proprietorship* may be the best way to go, since everything relating to the business, from ownership to starting up to tax preparation is relatively simple. Sole proprietorships are easy to launch, are free from the intrusion caused by partners, directors or stockholders, and in most cases will give you some degree of relief when it comes to taxation and regulatory hassles.

There are some major drawbacks to partnerships and sole proprietorships, however. For example:

1. They do nothing to legally limit your liability or protect your personal assets from plaintiffs, should you ever be subject to a lawsuit.

2. They provide no type of separate legal entity that survives you; that is, when you die, the business (or your share in it) dies with you.

Corporations are sort of like paper monsters that have the power to do business, incur liabilities, acquire assets and enter into contracts on their own behalf, independent of the people who created them. Useful though it may be to have a corporation, you need to ask yourself: In my own situation, is a corporation really necessary?

## Limiting your liabilities and losses

Exposure to liability is one of the principal reasons that people choose to incorporate their businesses. However, taking out an appropriate insurance policy may give you same or even more protection.

Nearly every profession or business classification has its own version of liability insurance. In my case, I carry an *errors and omissions* policy that protects me from being sued by clients or job-seekers who feel that my professional advice led directly to some mishap or tragedy. On paper at least, my corporation should protect me. But in this age of legal lunacy, I feel it's impossible to have too much protection when your livelihood is at stake.

To find out what sort of insurance needs suit your particular venture or occupation, contact a reputable business insurance agent. Very possibly, there's no potential for liability in your line of work; but if there is, it would be silly to lose your home, your health and your business when a disaster could be avoided with the proper insurance.

Just to play it safe, you should also protect your physical property from loss. Inventory, documents, files (both paper and electronic), computers, furniture and equipment can all be underwritten with a small business insurance policy. If you have walk-in traffic, this type of policy will also provide premises liability coverage, which protects you from slip-and-fall cases, as well as building coverage (if your space is leased).

If you own a restaurant, retail store, service station, garage or contracting business, your liability is also covered under most small business policies.

And for additional protection, you should definitely consider a disability policy, especially if you have a high-density career, in which your day-to-day work activities translate into your sole source of income.

## The health insurance dilemma

In terms of your personal and family health insurance needs, there are a bewildering number of options available, none of them, in my opinion, adequate or reasonably priced in relation to the value received. And now that the insurance industry is scrambling to anticipate the effects of health care reform, no one can predict what lies ahead for the self-employed. All we can do is hope that things will get better.

If you've recently left an employer, my advice would be to get off your COBRA plan while you're healthy; otherwise, you'll be at risk down the road when your eligibility expires.

For those of us with less than unlimited resources, the position we've been forced into by private insurers is to trade a higher deductible for a lower premium. In other words, the insurance goal of the '90s is not to provide coverage, but to protect against catastrophic illness or accidents.

I would welcome the opportunity to join an HMO, but unfortunately, in the state I live, HMO policies aren't offered to individuals, so a group health plan isn't even an option.

Many trade and political organizations offer insurance plans to their members. These sorts of deals, though, should be scrutinized very carefully. While many are undoubtedly on the up-and-up, I've heard of horror stories surrounding cancellation, slow payment or nonpayment of benefits by carriers selling "discount" insurance products to unsuspecting groups.

Expensive as it is to work with a first-rate or reputable carrier, my experience has shown that you usually get what you pay for. When evaluating insurance for your business or family, remember what they used to say on the TV show "Hill Street Blues": "Be careful out there."

———◆———

*The better you control your costs,
your image and your legal protection,
the more likely you'll be to succeed.*

# Chapter 9

◆

# Mastering the Sales and Marketing Game

◆

I look at sales and marketing as a kind of football game, in which you, the seller, are the offense, and the customer, or buyer, is the defense.

According to *My Rules of Sports*, the more points the offense scores, the more it benefits the defense. Sure, it's the defense's job to prevent the offense from scoring, but in the end, the defense feels a certain dysfunctional satisfaction from letting the offense score.

Anyway, in our imaginary football game in which the Bears play the Lions (the Bears being the sellers and the Lions being the buyers), the Bears, as is customary in football, go into a huddle at mid-field to call a play they think will work against the Lions.

"Let's throw the ball," the Bears' quarterback whispers to his teammates, as he glances over at the slouching defense. "We're taller than they are, and catching it won't be a problem for our receivers."

"OK," whispers back the wide receiver. "Once I catch the ball, I'll be able to run to the end zone and score a touchdown."

So the Bears line up and snap the ball. The quarterback drops back to pass, and lofts a perfect spiral toward the outstretched hands of the wide receiver, who's already got six points on his mind.

Suddenly, from out of nowhere, a Lion defender leaps unbelievably high and deflects the ball at the last second, and the play is called dead.

## Leaping meatballs

Back in the huddle, the Bears mull over what went wrong.

"Rats," groans the quarterback, as he shoots a chilly stare at the wide receiver and spits on the turf. "We ran a really great pattern and I threw a strike right at your hands. What went wrong?"

"I guess the Lions are better leapers than we thought," admits the wide receiver. "So a pass play may not be the way to score a touchdown."

"Well, then, let's try something different, since throwing the ball obviously isn't going to work. Any ideas?"

"How about a running play?" barks the fullback. "We're stronger and heavier than they are, and we can push those meatballs around all day. I'm sure we can score a touchdown if we just run the ball up the middle."

And so it goes in the marketing and sales game, a crucial aspect of yours and every business. Marketing is simply the strategy you use in order to make a sale. Or, using the football analogy, marketing is the play you call that you hope will score a touchdown. Bear in mind that your strategy is only good if it gets the results you want. You may call a beautiful-looking play in the huddle, only to find that the play is ill-suited in relation to the resistance of the other side. You can't assume, for example, that just because you're tall, the strategy you devise will automatically result in a touchdown; you may discover that the other side can easily compensate by their ability to jump.

## Marketing is a snap

Like the quarterback of the Bears, you need to size up the defense before you call each play, maximizing what works and minimizing what doesn't. Believe me, lots of perfectly good products die on the vine each year for lack of a sound marketing plan. Fortunately, though, every time the ball is snapped, you get another opportunity to make a sale; just remember that marketing doesn't exist in a vacuum—ultimately, everything hinges on the receptivity or resistance of the other side.

As a seller, then, it's important to put yourself in the position of the buyer, and ask these questions in regard to the product or service you're trying to sell:

*Do I need it? Do I want it?*

*Can I afford it? Will I use it?*

And then,

*If I buy it, when will I buy it,*
*how often will I buy it,*
*and in what quantity will I buy it?*

or,

*If I won't buy it, why?*
*What has to change*
*that will make me want to buy it?*

When you run a play—excuse me, market your product or service—you're probing for the answers to these questions, which, by the way, relate directly to a significant portion of the business plan you wrote. Marketing can also be done proactively. This is especially true in large corporations, whose marketing departments, through the use of surveys, focus groups, intuition or dumb luck, strive to anticipate the needs of the consumer, or in effect, find the parade already in progress and worm their way in front of it. Sometimes, as in the fashion industry, the public is *told* what it wants; but generally speaking, marketing involves the anticipation and/or reaction to consumer trends, even those that are buried in the collective subconscious.

One of the most striking books on the subject of marketing is *The Popcorn Report*, written by Faith Popcorn, founder of the BrainReserve, a consulting firm that predicts consumer behavior for Fortune 500 companies. Ms. Popcorn and her brain reserve are the frighteningly insightful trend spotters who've coined such terms as *cocooning, egonomics* and *cashing out,* concepts that have played a vital role in helping big companies understand where the action (translation: money) is in every imaginable modern-day product or service. To anyone wishing to get a glimpse into marketing science taken to a staggering level of sophistication, then consider *The Popcorn Report* required reading.

## The tried and the true

A successful marketing strategy will result in sales activity. If you're not achieving the sales volume your plan calls for, then it's time to go back to the huddle and call a different play before you snap the ball again.

The marketing strategies we're going to discuss in this chapter are the tried-and-true vehicles that businesses have been using for years to generate sales. Some may work for you, and others may not. If they don't, you may have to tweak them occasionally to get results. For example, just because a display ad in a newspaper isn't boosting sales the way you'd hoped, that's no reason to assume that all display advertising doesn't work. It may mean that your product or service is best marketed through a different sort of publication, say a trade magazine or newsletter. If nothing seems to generate sales, then the problem may be your product or service itself. Remember, no amount of marketing was able to sell the Edsel—the car simply had no appeal at the time it was introduced.

Let's assume, though, that your product or service idea is essentially sound, and has the inherent ability to generate sales. One of the most basic and effective marketing techniques is direct mail. I'm going to spend a lot of time talking about direct mail for two reasons: First, it can be one of the most rewarding ways to make money with a minimum of investment; and second, direct mail's fundamental principles are transferable to other types of media. For example, if you can design a solid direct-mail piece that pulls in business, then chances are you'll be able to put together an effective display ad or radio commercial. By the same token, if you understand the theory behind mail list management, you'll automatically be ahead of the game when it comes to mounting a tele-marketing campaign.

# Direct-mail bonding

Direct mail is the technique of approaching customers by way of their mailboxes. Millions of businesses use direct mail as either the sole means of attracting customers (as in the catalogs of Lillian Vernon), or in tandem with other types of advertising (as in VISA or American Express, who use television and print ads to appeal to new prospects).

Direct mail to me is the cat's meow. With the right product and a properly executed campaign, you can live the dream of sitting at home and watching your mailbox fill up with checks. *Yes!*

Sales transactions generated from direct mail may occur at a local retail outlet or point of service; or be delivered via the post office or delivery service to the customer from the seller's manufacturing facility or distribution center. *Drop shipping* occurs when the seller acts merely as a representative of the manufacturer, and upon receipt of the customer's order, instructs the manufacturer to deliver the product directly to the customer. In many mail order businesses, the *fulfillment* function (filling the order) can be handled by the seller or by a third-party fulfillment house, specialized in the inventory, warehousing, packaging and delivery of the product.

For example, if you were to publish a newsletter, it may be more than you could handle to process new subscriptions and then sort, staple, bundle and bag 5,000 newsletters at your kitchen table and schlep them down to the post office. In such a case, you'd probably want to turn over the fulfillment part of your business to someone else.

# The call to action

The goals of direct mail can vary considerably, depending on your customers and the type of product or service offered. Generally speaking, the *response* you're seeking will fall into two categories. Either you want the customer to pick up the phone (or fill out a form or run to the nearest retail outlet) and place an order immediately, or you want the customer to request additional information that you hope will result in a sale at a later date.

Retail products and services can make an immediate impact with direct mail. That is, their call to action can be answered quickly and in person by the customer, and the results of a direct mail marketing campaign can be tracked fairly easily.

Big-ticket items or intangibles, however, have a longer selling cycle by nature, and are more difficult to track. The call to action with an expensive offering usually relates more to the request for additional information than it does to an immediate sale. Hardly anyone I know, for example, has the cash on hand or the credit limit available to pick up the phone and order a single engine plane or a burial plot at Forest Lawn in response to a direct-mail solicitation.

## Defining your target market

Direct mail can take many forms and target a variety of customers. A chimney sweeping service making a general solicitation, for example, may send out 3 million letters to all the home owners in Atlanta, while a company offering a new metal polishing compound may send out as few as 1,000 letters to coin collectors in North America who belong to an elite numismatic society.

Not surprisingly, a sort of commercial symbiosis has evolved between big-time direct-mail marketers and professional demographers, who've developed a codependency as entangled as that between politicians and pollsters or underwriters and actuaries. Since it only makes sense to solicit business from those in a position to buy, demographers (employed by market research firms, ad agencies or the census bureau) have had a field day identifying to sellers the most likely prospects.

With the explosion (some would say exploitation) of accessible information detailing our personal incomes, buying habits, education, age and so forth, it's not surprising that resourceful demographers can accurately pinpoint for direct-mail clients which consumers in precisely which zip codes will most likely buy what products. Demographers have even authored a certain insider jargon to describe specific types of prospects, and their descriptions can be considered either hilarious or insulting, depending on the degree to which you consider the stereotyping of America according to purchasing tendencies to be a cultural turn for the worse.

For example, are you a member of the buying suburban subset known as the *pools and patios*, or do you belong to the less affluent group, *shotguns and pickups*? Are you a *belonger*, an *achiever*, an *emulator*, a *societally conscious* consumer, or a *need-driven* American? No need to answer—a demographer already has you pegged in a certain buying zone. Which makes perfect sense. After all, why would a direct-mail marketer waste time sending a Land's End catalog to a shotgun-and-pickup household, or a trial subscription to *Guns & Ammo* to a pools-and-patios address?

Many people object to the way demographic information is gathered and disseminated, and consider it an intrusion of privacy. And for years to come, the debate over its proliferation will continue to rage, as demographers dutifully make their correlations between age and pet food selection, income and airbag preference and gender and dental floss flavorings.

But undeniably, the more that's known about a population and its infrastructure of buying tendencies, the more cost effective and profitable direct mail will become, and the more valuable its potential for your own breakaway business.

## Lust for the list

The *list*, then, becomes the all-important element in the design of a direct-mail campaign. Lists, however, need not represent the culmination of a demographer's complicated calculus. Lists can simply consist of the obvious prospects for whatever you're selling. With a little imagination, you can come up with a profile of those people who are the most likely to buy—or in other words, those who are worth the investment of your mailing.

As long as you can imagine who your best prospects are, you can obtain or create a list that will enable you to reach them, whether they're consumer or business-to-business prospects. Think for a minute. What might they all have in common? Do they all subscribe to a certain magazine? Work as purchasing managers at drug stores? Live in high-rent neighborhoods? Belong to specific trade organizations? Attend the same schools or have the same religious denominations? Work in the same professions? Own the same brand of car? Use the same credit card? Eat at the same restaurant? Enroll their children in the same day-care centers?

Once you know your buying population, you can acquire a list in one of several ways. You can either build the list yourself, if you have the time and inside track to compile the names and addresses. Or, you can purchase a list from an independent list broker who either specializes in certain fields or compiles data from public sources such as the yellow pages or industry directories like Standard & Poor's or Dun & Bradstreet. You usually have a choice of receiving mailing labels or floppy disks containing the names you want (and arranged the way you want, either alphabetically or by zip code); and in some cases, lists are available on-line or in CD-ROM formats.

Since I deal mostly in the business-to-business realm, I've entered into a licensing agreement with MarketPlace Business of Cambridge, Massachusetts. They supply me with a list of more than 7 million companies nationwide, updated on a quarterly basis. Since the list is on a CD, I can search through it for prospects fairly quickly, either by name, geographic location, phone number or size of company (number of employees or annual sales). Best of all, the companies' products or services are all profiled according to an eight-digit standard industrial classification (or SIC code). With this degree of specificity, I can create a mailing list of companies in Arkansas that say, make at least $5 million worth of automotive gaskets annually.

Another alternative is to skip the brokers and work directly with the publishers themselves. In addition to the lists obtainable from the phone company, the chamber of commerce and the publishers of industrial and trade directories, many magazines and newsletters offer their subscription lists to direct mailers for a fee, which varies according to the number of times you wish to use the list and the quality of the prospects. A list containing the name of the president of each company will naturally cost more than a list of companies addressed, "President" or "General Manager."

## Mail list equality

My preference is to trade lists with other direct mailers, or barter for lists. For example, I recently obtained an alphabetized list of the 1,500 subscribers of a technical magazine in exchange for a two-part editorial the magazine had asked me to write.

When it comes to direct mail, however, all lists are not created equal. Assuming the lists are clean, the most valuable lists are, in decreasing order, the ones that contain the names of:

- Past buyers of your product, especially those who've made purchases recently.
- Past buyers of similar products.
- Potential buyers who are qualified by their potential to want your product.
- Unknown buyers, or generic prospects who may or may not be interested in what you have to offer.

Lists, like baseball cards, vary considerably in their worth to the knowledgeable collector, and quality will often counterbalance size in the quest for the perfect list. So when making a deal, be careful not to trade a Babe Ruth for a dozen Steve Balbonis. You might end up getting burned.

## Direct-mail hygiene

The downside to direct mail is that as quickly as it can fill your mailbox with checks, it can also fill your mailbox with bills. When that happens, you know your direct mail has become *junk mail,* which is the definition of direct mail that doesn't work. Junk mail is an offering that doesn't "connect" with the recipient to provide a pleasurable shopping experience, and becomes a nuisance that ends up in the trash, giving you *nada* in return for your investment.

To ensure that the mail you send creates an impact, not a landfill, try to observe the following rules of list maintenance:

- *Build* your list by continually adding fresh names. Otherwise, you'll wear out your welcome and your list will become stale.
- *Clean* your list by removing duplicated names, deleting unwanted names, correcting the spellings of names (a huge turnoff to prospects) and adjusting or deleting names in response to relocation. This ongoing process is called *list hygiene* in the trade, and it's one of the most important canons of direct mail.

- *Test* your list by sending out mail to a small sample portion at first. If you get a bad return, drop the list or make other adjustments before you send more money down a black hole. If you get a favorable response, then you know your investment is going to pay off, and you can crank the mailing up to full volume.

- *Code* your lists if you mail more than one at a time. Otherwise, you may not be able to identify where you're getting your returns from. To code a list, add a superfluous item to your return address, such as "Dept. D," or "Suite 101." The postal service will still deliver the response back to you, and you'll know which list is working. For phone orders, ask the person placing the order where he or she saw the offering; otherwise, you won't know if the response was prompted by a referral or a display ad.

- *Seed* your list. This is a sneaky way to protect your list from theft. Plant your own name, a pseudonym or the name of a friend in an inconspicuous place on your list. That way, if you sell or trade your list to someone else for a single run only and you start to receive repeat mailings, you'll have conclusive evidence the person you handed your list to is cheating.

Naturally, a totally raw list may be impractical or too cumbersome to own. For example, if you've purchased a list of 300,000 prospects in Tulsa in the hope that they'll buy your water purification system, then it makes sense only to record the names of those who respond. On the other hand, if your "universe" (that is, the total number of potential buyers) is relatively small (say, Ivy League physicists under the age of 30 who live in Kansas), then ownership of the entire list would be well-advised, and well within your means.

## Direct-mail mathematics

Which raises the issue: How many names do you need in order to launch a successful mailing? Well, the answer varies depending on the quantity and dollar value you need from your return in order to recover your costs and turn a profit.

Generally speaking, the industry standard acceptable rate of response is around 2 percent. So if you make two sales for every 100 direct-mail pieces sent, you're doing OK. Knowing the 2-percent rule should help you estimate how big your mailing should be to break even, if you figure in the cost of the product itself plus the cost of the list, the copy writing, the artwork, the printing, the postage and the fulfillment (which includes the packaging, shipping, handling, insurance and credit card fees.)

One thing to keep in mind: There is a lower limit to how much you should charge for your product. Most experts put the price minimum at around $20 or $25 per unit, unless you're selling via a catalog, in which case, you should still require a minimum order. If you sink below $20 or so, then your profit margin in a direct-mail campaign is likely to scrape bottom.

Remember, too, to collect taxes if applicable and shipping and handling charges, unless these are built into your price (I did this with my books—it made the offer more attractive to say, "price includes shipping and handling," both from a psychological and a logistical aspect).

## The list, the piece and the offer

List management has become a science in the world of business, particularly when the list becomes integrated into a full-scale electronic data base, which can be fully utilized for a variety of purposes, including marketing, customer analysis, sales tracking, invoice generation, accounting, purchasing, inventory control, distribution, customer service, and so on.

Just remember that the list, though absolutely critical, is only one variable in the algebra of direct mail. The other two variables are the *piece* itself and the *offer*.

No matter how wonderful and attractively priced your product or service, if your piece is weak, your response will be weak, too. By the same token, a beautifully designed piece will languish if your product or price offer is undesirable.

Although direct-mail pieces can vary considerably according to the market, product and imagination of the seller, all strong pieces have several things in common.

First, they must be attractive and easy to understand. The last thing you want is for the prospect (who you spent so much time and money trying to reach) to puzzle over the piece of mail in his or her hand and not "get it." Whether the piece is a postcard, a self-mailer, a letter, a catalog or a glossy brochure, your message should run as clear as a trout stream in Alaska—not polluted in a babble of ambiguous messages.

Second, a piece should have a "hook" or attention grabber that compels the prospect to open the piece and read what's inside. "You may already be a winner!" and "Open here for details of your free trip to Bermuda" are familiar, tried-and-true hooks.

Third, a piece has to offer the prospect several benefits of ownership. Later, when we talk about benefit selling, you can start to understand your prospects' needs (and how they'll help you score a touchdown).

Fourth, a piece must demand the prospect's participation in a call to action. "Call toll-free now!" or "Yes! Start my one-year subscription to *Warlords of the World!* (And bill me in four monthly installments of only $39.95)" are a couple of the clichés of the trade commonly used to mobilize the prospect into placing an order.

Lastly, a strong piece will enable the prospect (soon to be a *customer*) to easily make a purchase. By providing an attractive order form that's easy to fill out (or a pleasant voice on the phone), you can make the process of buying enjoyable, rather than a hassle.

## How to reduce your costs

One way to significantly reduce the cost of direct mail is to get a bulk mail (third-class) permit from the U.S. Postal Service. Just bear in mind that it takes a minimum number of pieces per mailing to achieve any degree of savings. In addition to the annual fee of $60, you must factor in the time and hassle involved in preparing your mailing in such a way as to meet a slew of bureaucratic standards. This requires not only the tedium of hand-sorting and bundling your mail according to zip code, but also waiting in line at the main post office (your local branch generally isn't set up to process bulk mail) to have it weighed. I've found that in direct-mail runs of less than several thousand units, it's just as cost effective to send mail first class.

Cooperative mailings can also provide you with an economical means of marketing your product or service. Basically, there are two types of cooperative mailings, in which several companies with similar markets share the costs of a single mailing:

1. *Card decks.* These are hermetically sealed stacks of postcard-size pieces, most often used in business-to-business marketing. Quick and to the point, card deck pieces are usually printed in black ink on white card stock, and have little aesthetic appeal. Their goal is to arouse sufficient interest in the prospect to generate an inquiry.

2. *Letter stuffers.* These are envelopes containing several companies' direct-mail pieces, plus any brochures, price lists or supplemental materials that wouldn't normally be sent as part of a direct-mail campaign.

Let's suppose you were in the business of selling pencils and pens in bulk to customers in downtown offices. If you were to join forces with 10 other providers of office supplies, you could send out a cooperative mailing at one-tenth the cost. Your mailing would appeal to the market you serve in much the same way as a catalog. The difference is, you have much more flexibility and less production expense in a card deck or letter stuffer format than with a catalog.

## Samplers, fliers and inserts

Despite the fact that direct mail is the most prevalent approach to direct marketing, there are a number of other efficient means of making direct customer contact. Known as *alternate distribution systems*, these strategies make use of delivery techniques other than the mail.

Since it's illegal for anyone other than the U.S. Postal Service to put something in a mailbox, you can use door-to-door samplers, a particularly cost-effective method of blanket coverage where a minimum of 10,000 prospects need to be reached. (A typical price for a sampler is four cents per unit.) In rural areas in which door-steps or doorknobs aren't easily accessible, a drive-by "hook and nail" attachment to mailboxes will insure delivery to each targeted household.

According to the Door Store, an alternate distribution marketer in the Midwest, door-to-door samplers are delivered to an average of 600,000 households a week in the Cincinnati area alone. Most of the samplers are put together by several sellers on a cooperative basis, referred to in the direct marketing industry as "marriage systems." (See a good example of an insert on the next page.)

Other types of direct marketing strategies include the use of fliers, which can be passed out in public areas or placed on the windshields of parked cars. I used the flier approach when I was in high school as a means of attracting customers to my house painting business. I simply walked around affluent neighborhoods looking for houses that needed a fresh coat of paint and slipped a flier under the door. For a couple of summers, I had more work than I could handle.

Not to be overlooked is the effectiveness of the insert, a now-ubiquitous feature of every Sunday newspaper and most major magazines. My wife counted no less than eight inserts in a recent issue of *Ladies' Home Journal* paid for by marketers hawking everything from a Norman Rockwell "canvas reproduction" framed in genuine oak to a limited-edition Elvis commemorative plate high-fired in fine porcelain.

While it's sometimes hard to resist the temptation to poke fun at products such as these, I have to give the marketers a great deal of credit. Believe me, if they weren't making lots of money, they wouldn't be investing in these types of inserts.

Another common insert strategy is to either cross-sell, resell, or up-sell to your current customers. Open any magazine, and look at the first thing that falls to the floor; more than likely, it's a subscription offer. Similarly, the wise direct marketer will always include a catalog or new product announcement in any package shipped. The next time you get a credit card statement, take a look at all the inserts and attachments that came with it. Writing checks is bad enough, but do we really have to make a career out of tearing off all the little Franklin Mint and Mickey Mouse watch flaps on the window envelopes?

*Figure 9.1: An effective insert from a cooperative door-to-door campaign.*

Sure, we all complain. But maybe there's something to be learned from the efficiency and (I assume) the profitability of this type of marketing. The next time you send an invoice, stick a marketing piece in the envelope. Heck, you've already paid for the postage; why not do a little fishing while you've got your customer's attention?

# The world of telemarketing

The term telemarketing has earned a terrible reputation lately, mostly as a result of the stereotypic rude, pushy and intrusive callers determined to sell us any number of items, especially at dinner time. Consumer backlash against the bombardment of telephone solicitation has gotten so intense that it's spawned a technological defense, the Caller ID (which, in a supreme irony, is a product already being pitched by annoying telemarketers).

However, as with direct mail, telemarketing has proven to be so effective that it's become an irresistible marketing vehicle to an infinite array of businesses. Telemarketing activity generally falls into one of two categories:

- *Discrete telemarketing* is performed directly by the seller or seller's agent, and involves the marketing of a big-ticket, complex or customized product or service whose acceptance hinges on a personal relationship between the caller and the buyer. Stockbrokers, insurance agents, financial planners and a wide variety of consultants use discrete telemarketing to prospect for new business over the telephone, aware of the fact that their success is usually dependent on a combination of personal qualities such as specialized skill, persistence and the ability to build trust with the customer.

- *High-volume telemarketing,* on the other hand, is less dependent on the personal and professional qualities of the caller. Rather, its success is more a function of the sheer number of calls made. Products and services that are easily understood by the prospect and that have a short selling cycle (or impulse purchase potential) are particularly well-suited to high-volume telemarketing. Not surprisingly, charitable and special-interest organizations, as well as suppliers of credit cards, magazine subscriptions and long-distance services rely heavily on telemarketing as a sales generation technique.

The goals of telemarketing can be very similar to those of direct mail: It is hoped that each call will result either in an order or a request for more information. One common goal of high-volume telemarketing is to set up an appointment with a salesperson who will close the deal at home or at the office, or at the very least, further qualify the prospect in person.

## The ultimate numbers game

Some large companies have their own in-house telemarketing departments. Most companies, though, rely on independent telemarketing firms or freelancers to help them design and execute telephone campaigns.

If you're considering a high-volume telemarketing campaign, remember that effectiveness, cost and versatility vary widely throughout the industry. Many large firms have minimum fees of around $1,000; but the tradeoff is that they're more likely to be equipped with state-of-the-art, computerized dialing systems designed to enhance calling volume, target only the telephone exchanges you want and avoid duplications and/or misdialings.

Large telemarketing companies will also help you write a "script" and test-market it along with several variations to pinpoint the most effective phraseology needed to market your product or service. Sounds like direct mail, doesn't it? *The list, the piece, the offer.*

Telemarketing serves a number of business purposes other than the direct solicitation of business. For example, I've used telemarketers in the role of researchers in order build a list of potential customers. The script we devised asked small to medium-sized companies to verify their current addresses and, by the way, reveal the names of their presidents, sales managers and engineering directors.

Since telemarketers tend to be versatile by nature, many companies use them to follow up on forgotten customers, survey new prospects for product receptivity, and perform simple customer service and public relations functions.

As in direct mail, you should calculate your telemarketing return rate so as to turn a profit. In contrast to direct mail, your investment doesn't involve copywriting, artwork, printing or postage. As someone who's made a living during the last decade as a discrete telemarketer, I can attest to the value of a good script, an accurate list and a valuable offer. If getting on the phone isn't your thing, though, you can always pay someone else to do the blocking and tackling and set the stage for your touchdown.

Direct marketing is the ultimate numbers game. There's money to be made, as long as you can keep the percentages in your favor and crank out lots of mail, samples, fliers, inserts or calls.

---

*Your business success is directly related to your mastery of the marketing game.*

◆

# Chapter 10

# Getting Results from Advertising & Promotion

◆

Advertising is a slippery science at best. A well-planned campaign can make you a fortune overnight; or for no apparent reason, bring about your financial ruin. The power of advertising is such that a slogan, mascot, motto or image that strikes a chord with the consumer can indelibly inscribe your product or corporate identity into our national cultural fabric.

Whether the campaign results in profits is another matter. For every ad campaign that succeeds (such as "Tastes great, less filling"), there's one that fails, like the California Raisin Growers' endearing "Heard it Through the Grapevine" claymation video (clever, yet ineffective in generating expected revenues).

Like any investment, it's best to carefully apportion your use of advertising, and allow for the fact that an effective ad campaign isn't cheap. Advertising costs can really add up, especially if you feel the need to sign up a celebrity spokesmodel or hire a high-profile ad agency to spruce up your image. Stories of expensive ad campaigns that either fizzled or had dubious goals abound. For example, when the U.S. Postal Service decided it needed a new logo in order to positively influence the public's perception of mail carrier efficiency, it hired the Madison Avenue firm of Young & Rubicam.

"We need to send a clear signal that we are dedicated to a new level of quality, customer focus and competitiveness," said Marvin Runyun, the Postmaster General. The result? A perfectly good logo was changed from a picture of an eagle next to the words "U.S. Mail" to the picture of an eagle next to the words "United States Postal Service"—at a cost of $7 million. (Maybe what the Postal Service really needed was to deliver the mail on time—now *that* would send a clear signal.)

## The list, the piece, the offer: Part 2

The point is, no amount of advertising can work the miracle of alchemy and change a lead product into gold. What advertising *can* do is:

- Put your product in front of potential buyers and extol its virtues.
- Reinforce your product's positive features to existing customers.
- Distinguish your product from the competition (even if no actual distinction exists).

As in direct mail, the success of your ad campaign depends on three basic factors: the list (in this case the target audience you identify), the piece (the ad itself) and the offer (the desirability of your product in the eyes of the customer, in terms of benefits and affordability).

In determining the target audience for your product, you need to identify the demographics of your ideal customer, and how they're most easily reached. Are they a population defined by such things as geography, income, age, gender or buying habits? If so, there's a medium out there that's tailor-made to tap them on the shoulder.

## The best media selection

In advertising, the better your choice of media (and the more focused it is on your specific audience), the more likely your success. Luckily, there are many types of media from which to choose, each with the potential for hitting a home run.

A textbook example of a medium, a market and an advertiser hitting on all cylinders is the phenomenon of daytime television, in which melodramas like "As the World Turns" and "General Hospital" evolved into perpetual cash engines for sponsors. Nicknamed *soap operas* because of their close association with the behemoth cleanser manufacturer Procter & Gamble, they shrewdly bored in on a population consisting of homemakers in a position to buy products such as Tide, Crest and Cheer.

Aside from the demographic makeup of each type of media, the most critical aspect of advertising centers around the potential for coverage. But how do you know exactly the size of the audience you're trying to reach? Well, in the print media, for example, most publishers provide semi-annual circulation statements in which the actual paid and nonpaid counts are provided. To ensure the accuracy of the circulation figures provided by the publishers, non-profit audit bureaus (working under the auspices of the advertisers, the ad agencies and the publications themselves) issue yearly reports, documenting the geographical circulation statistics as well as a *source analysis*, a general demographic accounting of the readership.

The two major U.S. audit bureaus are the Business Publications Audit of Circulation International (referred to in the trade as the BPA) and the Audit Bureau of Circulation (or ABC). Smaller bureaus include the Verified Audit Circulation Corporation and the Magazine Publishers of America (or MPA), which specializes in magazine circulation; and for foreign circulation figures, there are a half-dozen other reputable auditors.

Business publications usually provide a profile of the business and occupational backgrounds of their readership for the benefit of advertisers concerned with the demographics of their prospective customers. If you're scrutinizing the circulation figures of a business publication, don't be put off if most of the subscriptions are nonpaid. *Controlled-circulation* business and technical magazines generate their revenues from the sale of advertising, rather than the subscription price collected from the sale of each issue. As a result, business publishers take great pains to make sure that their publications end up in the hands of "high-quality" readers, those who are most likely to buy the advertisers' products. To receive a nonpaid publication, prospective subscribers are usually required to complete a qualifying questionnaire before they're added to the rolls.

# Standard rates and data

Audit bureaus play an important role in the advertising game, according to Bill Fahy, a publishing consultant in Beverly, Massachusetts. "Without their audits, there's no way to verify the size or quality of each publication's list." However, Bill also points out that in highly specialized fields of interest, audits aren't always necessary, since the readership is assumed to be stable and homogeneous.

The most accessible wellhead of information regarding advertising rates, demographics and circulation comes from the Standard Rate and Data Service of Wilmette, Illinois. Publishers of more than 30 advertising and business reference books, the SRDS provides a wealth of relevant statistics to prospective advertisers in several comprehensive directories, including:

- *Business Publication Rates and Data,* a source book of more than 6,300 business, technical, trade, scientific and medical publications in the U.S. and Canada.
- *Consumer Magazine and Agri-Media Rates and Data,* a guide to advertising rates for magazines geared to the general readership.
- *Spot Television Rates and Data,* a listing of TV stations and markets nationwide, from the tiny Glendive, Montana, market with 4,560 viewers, to the enormous New York City market, with 7,043,740 viewers.
- *Spot Radio Rates and Data,* the Bible when it comes to investigating the cost of buying radio time in every U.S. market.
- *Newspaper Rates and Data,* the directory of all-purpose daily newspapers.
- *Community Publications Rates and Data,* a geographical compendium of weekly newspapers.
- A multitude of ethnic and special interest publications, including the *Hispanic Media and Markets Rates and Data.*

As you might expect, the cost of advertising is generally proportional to the size of the target audience, with the rate becoming more economical the greater the circulation. (Discounts are given for repeated runs, of course.) A quick glance through the *Business Publication Rates and Data* reveals the disparity of rates for a single-insertion, full-page black-and-white ad:

- *Knee Surgery* magazine, with a circulation of 2,251, charges $920 (40 cents per reader).
- *Meat & Poultry* magazine, with a circulation of 18,445, charges $2,350 (13 cents per reader).
- *Brake & Front End* magazine, with a circulation of 28,003, charges $3,915 (13 cents per reader).
- *U.S. News and World Report,* with a circulation of 2,319,553, charges $51,650 (2 cents per reader).

Since many large, national periodicals are published simultaneously for subscribers in different regions of the United States, it's possible to target a relatively narrow group of readers, with a proportionate cost reduction. For example, the price of a full-page ad in the Midwest version of *The Wall Street Journal* (circulation: 500,065) runs $36,248, while the same ad in the Detroit edition (circulation: 47,808) will cost a measly $6,269 per day.

## Trade shows and conventions

Many businesses swear by trade shows and conventions as a visible and cost-effective means of selling their products or services to a highly defined audience. As a vendor, you'll be charged a booth fee by the square foot or by a preset amount of space. If you reserve a space early, you can usually get a discount, and you can sometimes barter with the trade show sponsors for a reduction in price in exchange for presenting a seminar or demonstration to the attendees.

Your booth can be as simple as a table and a folding chair, or it can include audio or visual props that will help you attract buyers and display your wares in an aesthetically pleasing manner. Most trade show sponsors will minimally "dress" your space with a backdrop and an identifying sign, and for a reasonable cost, you can rent or buy attractive presentation "sets" from promotions suppliers or the convention promoters.

Detractors of trade shows consider them a waste of time and resources, based on the fact that historically, a large proportion of attendees lack the inclination or authority to make purchases. Equally dangerous to your business is the fact that trade shows expose you to your competition. "In the high-tech world, it's an open book," says Bill Moss, vice president of marketing for Computer Products, Inc., of Pompano Beach, Florida. "Exhibiting at a trade show is like voluntarily revealing the most intimate details of your products to all your competitors."

## Commerce or carnival?

Some trade shows have evolved into lavish bazaars in which the exhibitors compete for attention in an all-out war of budgetary and visual one-upmanship. It's no longer uncommon, for example, for single exhibitors to spend several hundred thousand dollars on elaborate booths that resemble futuristic stage shows featuring models, actors and celebrities.

If you're considering the trade show route, ask yourself if you can afford the investment of travel and exhibitor fees, and whether you can compete for prospective customers on a reasonable budget. As a rule, you should exhibit in shows in which the exhibitors (and attendees) are more interested in commerce than carnival. Otherwise, you might find it more beneficial to simply stroll the floor and hand out business cards than run off to join the circus.

To find the trade shows likely to attract your potential customers, look in the latest edition of *Trade Shows Worldwide*. It lists everything from the National Association of Pastoral Musicians convention (booth rental: $350 to $500) to the California Dental Association convention (booth rental: $1,400 to $1,500).

## Craft fairs: Politics as usual

Craft fairs are different than trade shows, in that they're specifically designed to make money for the artists. Most of the them are *juried*, which means that each artist's work is subject to the scrutiny of a panel before an exhibit booth is leased. A regrettable trend in craft shows, however, has been the charging of nonrefundable entrance fees to artists for the privilege of having to "audition" their work in front of judges, some of whom lack any artistic credentials or even a modicum of good taste. Sadly, the choice of who's granted a booth is often a highly political exercise, with even the most deserving artists finding themselves excluded from a field of "insiders."

Sponsors of craft shows (many of whom are municipalities or service organizations) have come to view the fairs as annual fundraisers for their own causes, and the price-gouging entrance and booth fees represent a blatant exploitation of artists, who generally make very little money for their efforts. Which is a real tragedy, in light of the immense sacrifice made by dedicated artists in their very personal pursuit of beauty and self-expression.

However, it *is* possible to make a decent living as a craft show exhibitor, as long as you have the stamina to lead a nomadic existence and haul your wares from one city to the next, week after week.

## Ad agencies: A 3-D perspective

If it looks like advertising is going to play a major role in starting, growing or maintaining your business, it might be wise to work with an agency. Agencies provide a variety of services, including everything from creative functions to market research to public relations. Agencies can help you define your corporate identity, and create communications materials such as logos, stationery, business cards, and so forth. Since they're well-connected with local subcontractors, they can usually find the best prices on printing, packaging, paper supplies and other materials.

A competent agency will help you plan the most effective campaigns, targeting only those media that are likely to get results. In terms of ad "placement," agencies generally receive a 15-percent discount from the media with which your ad is placed, but the savings aren't usually passed along to you; they're pocketed by the agency in the form of a commission, unless you negotiate with the agency up front to split the commission, and receive credit for the commission earned.

Agencies can be especially useful when developing complex campaigns or those involving specialized types of media, such as outdoor displays, billboards, bus placards and other types of signage.

Three-dimensional art can also present problems to the do-it-yourselfer, and may be best suited to the skills of an agency. This category of advertising includes point-of-purchase displays, window dressing, trade show displays and all types of distinctive product packaging. While most of us could probably come up with an adequate one-color design for something like a restaurant menu, a unique, four-color cardboard rack featuring two dozen custom-designed cookie boxes strategically placed at the supermarket checkout counter would represent a challenge on a totally different level.

## The third-party solution

You can work with an agency on an hourly or per-project basis when the project is sufficiently large—over several thousand dollars. Or, they may ask you to retain their services on a monthly or yearly contract basis. It most cases, it would be inadvisable for a fledgling business to agree to a retainer, for two reasons. First, you don't want to commit your resources before you've had a chance to see the actual return; and second, it would be foolish to sign a long-term agreement with someone who has yet to earn your trust. Besides, retained relationships have a high-stress probability built into them. Chances are, you'll either feel you're not getting what you paid for, or the agency will feel that they're overworked and underpaid for their efforts when the price is fixed and billed on a monthly basis.

Publicists and media placement specialists are like ad agencies, only their domain lies in attracting public attention, not placing advertising. If you're a Hollywood actor, for example, a good publicist will arrange television and radio interviews for you, alert the print media as to your comings, goings, signings, lawsuits and future appearances, and feed the tabloids with all the juicy details of your sex life with extraterrestrials.

Media placement people make sure your business stays on the front page, and will even ghost-write articles for you that will hopefully heighten the public's awareness of your existence (and keep your name in the news, even if there's nothing genuinely newsworthy about you).

An ad agency, publicist or media placement professional will only be able to help you if you or your product has some degree of merit or appeal. So again, be careful not to expect miracles from a third party when your business problem is fundamentally home-grown.

To test the waters (and save some money), you'd be well-advised to try some advertising and publicity on your own. That way, you'll not only bypass a potentially unnecessary middleman, you'll also gain some knowledge and first-hand experience, which will prove valuable should you decide to go the third-party route. In the beginning, call your own press conferences, issue your own press releases, write your own articles and design your own ad campaign. If you fail to get results, call in the experts. You might just find yourself making an immediate impact without betting the farm.

*In advertising and promotion, there are lots of ways to skin a cat.*

# Chapter 11

◆

# Sales Techniques for the Faint of Heart

◆

Hey, wouldn't it be great if we could all be like General Schwarzkopf? You know, kick some military butt, go in front of a TV audience of millions of admiring Americans, retire as a war hero, and then launch a lucrative breakaway career as an author, scholar, patriot and consultant? Heck, Stormin' Norman's got it made—and he didn't even have to send out invitations. The party came to *him*.

Don't think for a minute, though, that I'm trying to deprecate the achievements of a beloved four-star general, or begrudge him his success, because I'm not. I'm simply trying to make the point that mere mortals like ourselves can't expect the world to beat a path to our doors. Celebrity may be a wonderful commodity when launching a career, but most of us, I'm afraid, find it in short supply.

Aside from a few relatives, acquaintances and former co-workers, nobody much knows or even cares about your business aspirations, so you'd better get used to the idea of having an empty rolodex for a while. I've known a lot of people who've gone into business because their friends thought they had a terrific idea, but where were the friends six months later?

Of course it's great to have the encouragement of friends, as long as you remember that that's about all they can be counted on for. If you think your friends are going to help make you rich, just try selling to them, and see how fast they scatter. Like they say to new life insurance agents, in sales you run out of friends awfully quick.

The truth is, in order to take your business where you want to it go, you'll need to effectively explain the benefits of your product or service to a huge number of complete strangers, from creditors to customers. Or in other words, you'll need to learn how to sell.

## What is selling, anyway?

To a lot of people, the term *selling* paints an uncomfortable picture of coercion; or connotes some type of marginally criminal activity. Viewed as the dominion of used-car purveyors ("Have I got a deal for you..."), lawyers ("I think we can get your cousin, the serial killer, released on a plea bargain...") or politicians ("My fellow Americans, the time has come to raise your taxes..."), selling has gotten a bad rap, especially in the aftermath of the hog-wild '80s.

Selling isn't always the easiest or most pleasurable activity in the world for anyone, whether you're a retail clerk, a securities trader or a union negotiator. In my line of work, I can think of a lot more appealing things to do than pick up the phone to try to sell my services—like waiting in line to renew my driver's license on the last day of the month; or having my blood drawn to satisfy an insurance application. To be perfectly frank, most of the time I wish I could avoid the selling process altogether. But then again, I don't find poverty particularly appealing, either.

## Getting past the fear and loathing

So how do you overcome the fear and loathing of selling? Simple. You change both your definition and your approach.

Rather than look at selling as an adversarial endeavor or competition, try to look at selling as a *process* that involves the communication of information or ideas to another person. Period. If you can help the prospect see the benefit of what you're selling, great. If not, move on to someone else, or try back later.

117

Over the years, I've softened my approach to selling somewhat, and I've become less pushy. Call it confidence, or perhaps efficiency. Or call it the Golden Rule. I try to perceive the way *I'm* being perceived, and act accordingly. Since I hate the feeling of being *sold*, I try to avoid inflicting the pain on others.

Selling can be fun, especially when no one feels like it's happening. *Zen selling. What a concept.* When a sale does occur, it means the prospect has accepted the information or ideas you've presented as being beneficial, and a need has just been satisfied.

## The traditional selling dialect

Just like a language in which there are many dialects, selling, too, has many dialects, particularly when resistance or concern is encountered. Known in the trade as "objections," these stumbling blocks to sales can be handled in different ways, or with a variety of dialects.

Traditional selling methods encourage the seller to "overcome" objections with "rebuttals." Rebuttals are the responses (or arguments) a salesperson uses to influence the prospect's perception of need or willingness to make a purchase. Rebuttals are designed to either cast the seller's point of view in a more positive light or weaken the point of view of the prospect. Rebuttals are popular with sales trainers and sales managers within companies who teach their employees to memorize carefully scripted rebuttals to use whenever resistance is encountered. Often, "flip charts" containing rebuttals to common objections are provided, in case the front line salesperson's memory fails or he or she encounters an unusual objection that might require too much contemplation.

The objection/rebuttal method of handling resistance or concern is merely one dialect in the selling language. Communicating with your prospect in this dialect can be worthwhile, provided you both feel comfortable and productive.

## Overcoming objections vs. satisfying needs

A lot of changes have occurred in the selling profession recently. In order to become more responsive to an increasingly sophisticated, sales-resistant society, the selling profession has had to shift its emphasis away from *overcoming objections* towards *satisfying needs*. Many contemporary selling experts have found that the old-style objection/rebuttal dialect has serious limitations as an effective selling technique.

This is especially true of businesses that provide intangible services or sell big-ticket items, since the scope of each transaction is usually too complex to be trivialized or steamrollered by simplistic, insensitive rebuttals or hard-closing sales techniques. In my business, for example, where people's personal lives and careers are at stake, I have a responsibility to truly serve the best interests of my constituency, and in order to do so, I need to make a sincere effort to clearly understand everyone's concerns.

And from a purely practical matter, no one likes the feeling of being "hard-closed" by a self-serving salesperson. Such behavior, aside from being annoying, would ultimately be counterproductive, since hard-closers tend to turn off their customers after making the sale.

However, this doesn't mean that you should roll over and play dead each time your ideas meet with resistance. There's a way to best serve the interests of your prospects and continue to make sales.

## The power of client-centered selling

Nearly half a century ago, a prominent clinical psychologist named Carl Rogers (1902-1987) developed and perfected a method of counseling called "client-centered therapy." He discovered that by using a "nondirective" approach with his patients (or "clients"), he could produce rapid, beneficial results. By allowing the clients to freely discuss their feelings and concerns in an atmosphere of unconditional acceptance, Rogers was able to break down the usual fear, inhibition, and resistance that clients commonly associated with therapy.

The client-centered approach was unique in that it made no presumptions about the client's feelings or concerns, or how they should be handled. The therapist simply acknowledged his or her understanding of what the client expressed, and served as a neutral "sounding board."

Later, after years of research and clinical application, it was discovered that the client-centered techniques used in Rogers' approach to therapy could also be effectively applied to the fields of education, business management and selling.

"Client-centered selling" is a selling philosophy and application of techniques based upon the work of Carl Rogers. It gives the salesperson an alternative strategy to the traditional objection/rebuttal method of handling concerns, and helps break down sales resistance, allowing both the seller and the prospect to discover and openly discuss needs.

Once the prospect's needs are discovered, it becomes a simple matter to either satisfy them, or stop wasting each other's time.

# The nonconfrontational approach to selling

One of the most powerful forms of human interaction is empathy, since we all have the need to be accepted and understood by others. *Empathizing* is a way of showing another person that you understand his or her feelings or point of view, without necessarily agreeing, or expressing an opinion. In a verbal interaction with another person, empathy can be expressed three different ways: by acknowledging, paraphrasing and active listening. Here are the differences:

- *Acknowledging* is the mildest form of empathy, in which you simply let the other person know that you heard what he or she said. Phrases like, "uh huh," "sure" or "right," are common forms of acknowledging, and give the other person the green light to continue.

- *Paraphrasing* gives you the chance to communicate your understanding of what someone has said by restating it in your own words. This form of empathy allows the other person to correct you if you have somehow misunderstood him or her.

  For example, if the prospect tells you the cost of your illustration service is too high, you might paraphrase by saying, "In other words, the expense is simply beyond the limit of your budget." In this scenario, you're avoiding the temptation to argue; but on the other hand, you're not necessarily agreeing with the objection, either. You're just letting the prospect know you heard his or her concern, and you want the discussion to continue.

Paraphrasing is often confused with *parroting*, an old-style sales technique that goes something like:

"I want it in blue."
*"You want it in blue."*

*or*

"I can't afford it this year.
*"You can't afford it this year."*

Whatever you do, don't parrot back what someone says. Parroting is annoying and fails to show any understanding of what's been said.

- *Active listening* is the most powerful form of empathy, in that it summarizes the feelings and emotions of the other person. Like paraphrasing, it also gives the other person the chance to clarify their thoughts or correct your understanding of what's been discussed.

The key ingredient to any active listening statement is a "feeling word," which acts as a sort of emotional sounding board. For example, let's suppose a prospective client tells you that he doesn't think your bid for a particular job is competitive. You might empathize by saying, "You're disappointed by the price I gave you on my proposal."

The prospect then has the option of confirming or correcting your active listening (or "empathy") statement. For all you know, price wasn't the issue at all. Your prospect's concern may have centered instead on the delivery date, or the scope of services offered, or the payment terms.

By empathizing, you set the table for further discussions by assuming a noncombative posture of concern for the prospect's needs, rather than trying to shout down the other side and slam-dunk a sale.

Bear in mind that empathizing isn't selling; it's merely a technique you can use to lay the groundwork for selling by letting the prospect know that his or her concerns are understood.

# Putting client-centered selling to work

With a bit of practice, you can incorporate client-centered selling techniques into your everyday vocabulary. The next time you encounter a concern, follow this five-part formula:

1. Listen to the prospect's concern without interrupting.

2. Make an "empathy" statement, using an active listening response.

3. Check your understanding by listening carefully to the prospect's reaction.

4. Make a statement that describes the benefit of using your product or service, followed by a question that tests for acceptance.

5. Listen to your prospect's response.

Here's an example of how to handle a concern, using the five-part client-centered selling formula:

*Prospect:* I'm not sure I want to commit to a year-long contract with your computer maintenance service.

*You:* I see. You're afraid you might be disappointed with our technical expertise.

*Prospect:* Not at all. I'm concerned about the fact that you've only been in business for six months. For all I know, you'll fold up shop and leave us in the lurch.

*You:* I can see how you'd feel that way. However, my partner and I have a total of 27 years of continuous experience in the computer industry and have lived and worked in this area our whole lives. Wouldn't that give you more peace of mind than if you were to sign a contract with a big, impersonal firm from out of town that might be bought or sold at the whim of some financial executive?

*Prospect:*    Well, I never thought of that, but I guess you have a point.

You might be wondering whether empathizing in the client-centered selling format is always the best way to handle concerns. The answer is: No, of course not. It would be ridiculous to respond to simple, factual concerns by empathizing. Consider the following exchange that might occur in my line of work:

*Job seeker:*    Tell me again the total compensation package your client company is offering. It's not clear to me.

*Recruiter:*    You're *upset* with what they've given you.

*Job seeker:*    No, you dweeb, I *want* the job! Just tell me what the money is.

However, empathy, when used judiciously in a skillful and sincere manner, can do more for you in the long run than practically any other selling technique.

## Choosing dialects

Let's compare the traditional objection/rebuttal method with the client-centered approach when handling some universal objections. Remember that client-centered selling does nothing to directly answer or "overcome" objections, it merely increases the likelihood for further exploratory dialogue.

*Example one:*

**Prospect's objection:**    Your price is awfully high.

*Traditional response:*    Oh really? Compared to what?

*Client-centered response:*    It would be embarrassing to pay more than the going rate.

*Example two:*

**Prospect's objection:**    I don't think your company can do what I need.

*Traditional response:*    Well, we're certainly a lot more competent than the other bozos in town.

*Client-centered response:*    You may be unclear as to our capabilities. May I take a moment to explain some of our strengths in more detail?

*Example three:*

**Prospect's objection:**    You're late! You said you'd meet me here at 3:30 and it's nearly 4:00.

*Traditional response:*    Hey, chill out. What's so important about a stupid 15 minutes?

*Client-centered response:*    I don't blame you for being angry with me. Let's see if we accomplish what we need to in the time we have left.

*Example four:*

**Prospect's objection:**    We already have a lawn care service.

*Traditional response:*    Ah, yes, but my competitors use illegal chemicals that cause cancer in children.

*Client-centered response:*    It would be uncomfortable for you to switch to another service at this time. But I can assure you, with the type of economical, environmentally safe service we provide, it would be worth your time for us to chat.

There's no right or wrong way to handle objections. In fact, learning to become fluent in a variety of selling dialects will help increase your ability to satisfy needs. My experience as someone whose livelihood depends on selling fairly complex ideas to others has revealed that the objection/rebuttal method tends to put prospects on the defensive, fails to establish rapport and does little to discover needs or create need awareness. However, in your business, the objection/rebuttal method may work best.

When trust is a key factor, and you have the luxury of nurturing a long-term selling cycle, client-centered selling tends to work best, as it dissipates sales resistance, establishes rapport and encourages dialogue that's conducive to the discovery of needs.

## A balanced attack

The client-centered method is a more subtle means of persuasion, with its disadvantage being that it sometimes lacks the impact to get quick results. If making the sale *now* is of paramount importance, and you aren't overly concerned about developing or maintaining a business relationship, then the objection/rebuttal method is probably your best bet. Of course, if your prospects respond favorably to a harder-edged approach (as some invariably will), then by all means, go with the flow.

Naturally, you'll do your customers and your business a disservice if you fail to conceptualize the answers to common questions and concerns. In selling as in marketing, you should be well-versed (and even well-rehearsed!) in regard to your product's unique benefits or your company's competitive advantage.

It would be wise, in fact, to script out rebuttals or *recovery lines* to the resistance you're likely to encounter. You may not ever use them verbatim, especially if you take the client-centered approach, but just knowing the answers will help bolster your confidence and, in the process, make more sales.

The truth is, if you can't provide your prospects with powerful reasons for buying what you're selling, then you can't blame them for doing business with someone else. And the most powerful reasons of all have nothing to do with your product's features, and everything to do with their benefits.

## Feature-to-benefit conversion

Feature-to-benefit conversion is one of the most powerful aspects of the sales and marketing game, as it exposes human psychology as the open wound it is in relation to buying patterns. Your mastery of feature-to-benefit conversion will put you at the head of the class in terms of understanding the world of commerce, and will greatly enhance your ability to grow your business by selling to your customers' needs.

To begin, let's define some terms, according to Webster:

- *Feature.* A prominent or conspicuous part or characteristic. Power steering, power brakes and chrome wheels are *features* of an automobile.
- *Benefit.* Anything that is advantageous or for the good of a person. A feeling of comfort, safety and style are some of the possible *benefits* of power steering, power brakes and chrome wheels.

While a feature is *tangible* and can be looked at fairly objectively, the perception of what is beneficial is *intangible*, and highly subjective. When making a buying decision, each individual attaches a unique set of feelings to any given feature according to his or her perception of need. It's possible that a single feature can produce a wide range of emotional responses, depending on the observer.

Ownership of chrome wheels, for example, may induce a positive feeling of status, prestige or self-esteem in Fred; while the same set of wheels may spark feelings of individuality or aesthetic appreciation in Bob.

To John, however, chrome wheels may symbolize decadence, greed or vanity; and stir feelings of anger or resentment; while in the opinion of Stacy, chrome wheels indicate an added measure of road stability, and therefore satisfy a feeling of safety and security.

Clearly, then, a single *feature* is capable of arousing an infinitely wide spectrum of perceptions, or potential *benefits*. This phenomenon isn't lost on savvy selling professionals who know how to exploit the fact that a person will make a buying decision based on a product's perceived benefits, not for its features.

## Advertisers: The benefit masters

To learn how to convert features into benefits, look no further than the masters: advertisers. Paid for their ability to cleverly link up their clients' products with perceived benefits, advertisers make assumptions through market research (or, failing that, common sense) that the specific audience they're targeting will find the perceived benefits of their clients' products to be irresistible, and therefore desirable to own.

Ironically, some products have little or no distinguishable features to convert to benefits. In the case of *market-driven* products such as these, advertisers must rely on their skill in creating a powerful product-benefit association.

Beer companies, for instance, spend millions of dollars to produce television commercials. On a superficial level, these ads promote the rather commonplace features of their product: clear, crisp taste that's less filling, cold-filtered or genuine draft brewing, and so forth. Do consumers really care about (or purchase) beer for the way it's brewed? Absolutely not! People buy the advertisers' products because of the pleasurable feelings the "hidden persuaders" of television images and sound link to the products. Advertisers get us to associate their brand of beer with images of sexy men and women, sports heroes, warm friendships, family relationships and adorable, cuddly canines.

A more recent development in beer commercials has been the blatant appeal to the latent fears, prejudices and insecurities of the beer-consuming target audience by ridiculing or humiliating easy targets such as lawyers and Sumo wrestlers. The implication in all these types of TV commercials is that you and I will have feelings of sexiness, companionship, warmth or macho pride if only we were to run out and purchase the advertisers' products. Not too subtly, beer companies have spent years and fortunes in a campaign to subliminally sell a target market the perceived *benefits* of buying and consuming their particular brand of alcoholic beverage.

All of this is done, of course, without the viewer ever being shown the image of anyone actually drinking beer on television— those commercial images were banned by the FCC years ago! Yet the advertising tactic of linking product to pleasure helps fuel a multibillion dollar industry.

## Go boldly where the benefits lurk

To get the most impact when selling, see if you can convert the features of your product or service into benefits. Believe me, there's a benefit lurking behind every feature, even one as seemingly innocuous as price. To illustrate, consider the following scenario.

You've decided to offer a one-time discount to a new customer. On the surface, price is price. Big deal. But beneath the surface, the customer may experience a benefit from the discount in the form of certain positive feelings, such as:

- *Power,* because he got you to lower your price.
- *Control,* because he was able to work within his budget.
- *Relief,* because he now has enough money to pay his bills.
- *Smugness,* because you got something his friends or competitors were unable to get.
- *Security,* because he now knows he has a supplier he can count on to treat him fairly.

In some cases, you'll pick up a clue from the customer as to his or her buying motivation, or discover quite by accident what the underlying benefit of your product is to the customer. In other cases, you'll just have to take an educated guess, as Bill Levitt did in 1946.

According to David Halberstam in his book *The Fifties*, Bill Levitt, a 38-year-old home builder, bet the farm shortly after World War II that returning veterans and their families would experience an insatiable appetite to buy affordable, cookie-cutter homes in an outlying rural area within commuting distance of New York City. And he was right, in a big way.

But as it turns out, the enormity of the success of Levittown had little to do with the fact that there happened to be a post-war housing shortage. After all, Levitt could have built his homes anywhere.

No, what caused such a buying frenzy at Levittown (where as many as 1,400 houses were sold in a single day) was the fact that for the first time in history, young families were given the means to *move away from their parents.* Levitt had hit on a benefit so profound that it permanently changed the structure of American culture. Practically overnight, a home in suburbia became synonymous with realizing the American Dream.

Your business idea may not change the world, but it will definitely get a head start if you can understanding your customers' needs and the underlying benefits of your product or service. Selling need not be an exercise in deceit or futility, or an activity to be avoided. Selling can be fun. And the more it works, the more fun it becomes.

Whether or not you call "sales" your profession, you'll definitely need selling skills to get your business off the ground.

*The greater your ability to identify the needs of your customers, the more your business will prosper.*

# Chapter 12

# You're Worth the Money You Charge!

Not long ago, my wife and I found ourselves on the other side of town, so we decided to drop in on Ken, an old friend of mine. Luckily, he was at home.

Like me, Ken used to play jazz for a living full time, but now he's a successful breakaway entrepreneur. His first "regular" job after leaving the jazz life behind was for a company that sold the advertising that appears on plastic phone book covers.

After a few years of making money for someone else and punching a time clock, Ken struck out on his own, balancing his time between playing jazz, selling advertising and engineering audio and video projects on a freelance basis.

We hadn't seen Ken for several months, and when we arrived at his house, he eagerly led us down to the basement, which he'd been feverishly remodeling. When I saw the changes, I was in shock.

"Ken, this is unbelievable," I said, as I surveyed the gorgeous renovation. "The last time I was here, this place looked like a one-room cement box. Now it's been transformed into a five-room, air-conditioned office and fully equipped recording studio with wall-to-wall carpeting. This must have cost a fortune."

"Not really," replied Ken, with obvious pride. "See that 24-track mixing console in the studio? I traded a music store owner a big phone book cover ad for that."

"Not bad," I said.

"And see that ventilation system?" Ken pointed to the ceiling. "I had a heating and cooling company put that in free of charge, in return for a multiple insertion."

I had to admit I was impressed. "So you bartered your way to riches, so to speak."

"Right," said Ken. "Any time I needed a piece of equipment or some sort of building material, I just picked up the phone and cold-called a store owner. I guess all those years of telephone sales paid off, since I struck a deal on *every single call I made.*"

I was humbled. I couldn't remember *ever* batting a thousand. I made a mental note that it was time to brush up on my negotiating skills. Who knows, maybe someday I might want to remodel *my* basement.

We spent a pleasant afternoon with Ken, and when it was time for us to leave, he walked us out to the car. On the way, I happened to notice Ken's clean, newly poured concrete driveway.

"Ken, your driveway looks awful nice," I remarked. "You didn't by any chance..."

"Sure enough," said Ken. "Like they say, why pay retail?"

## Common sense and a little ingenuity

When we think of "negotiating," we sometimes picture smoke-filled rooms in which the fates and fortunes of hostages, highly paid athletes or striking steel workers are decided by high-powered special envoys, sports agents or court-appointed arbitrators.

But in reality, varying forms of negotiation are played out by every one of us on a continuous basis, in our family and social lives, and in our business relationships.

Negotiating is simply the process of helping people get what they want. And a skillful negotiator is someone who achieves a settlement that makes everyone happy.

The way in which Ken was able to remodel his basement illustrates how an effective negotiator can improve the quality of his or her life through using common sense and a little ingenuity.

In our business affairs, it's surprising to learn how many of us make needless concessions on a regular basis. These concessions can appear as discounted prices, unreasonable delivery schedules or the acceptance of poor quality supplies. Ironically, such unnecessary sacrifices are usually made in the spirit of "negotiating."

But making others happy at our own expense isn't negotiating; it's simply a way of avoiding the discomfort that comes from a potential disagreement, or the fear of turning away business. As a species, we have a congenital tendency to "go along," even if the result is counterproductive. And sadly, the cost to us in terms of lost revenues, increased anxiety, and weakened business credibility is enormous.

We have so much to gain and so little to lose by improving our negotiating skills. And the good news is that negotiating is neither painful nor difficult, once a few simple techniques have been mastered.

## We have met the enemy

My high school history teacher fought in the South Pacific during World War II. During his basic military training, U.S. soldiers were told countless stories of the unadulterated savagery and superhuman courage of their Japanese opponents. Make no mistake, the type of combat our troops were told to expect would be fierce, unrelenting and suicidal, according to the officers returning from duty.

"Evidently, the Japanese were given the exact same speech by *their* drill sergeants," my teacher chuckled. "Because the first time I came face to face with a Japanese soldier, we both practically jumped out of our skins!"

I like to relate this story to negotiating, because the "savagery" and "courage" of the other side is usually either overestimated or irrelevant. The important issues are your factual preparations, your mental attitude and the way in which you deal with new information. Walt Kelly's cartoon character *Pogo* probably describes most inexperienced negotiators when he says, "We have met the enemy, and it is us!"

So before you pull up a chair at the bargaining table, get a grip on your *own* needs, and what you realistically think is at stake. A good way to begin is to examine the arithmetic behind your own pricing structure, and how unseen nuances allow many of us to "negotiate" away chunks of money we're not even aware of.

For example, in a percentage-based fee business such as mine, a reduction in fee from 30 percent to 25 percent commission represents a discount of nearly *17* percent, not 5 percent. Translated into real money, on a placement of a $50,000 position, the difference is $2,500.

Early in my career, when I was less confident of my negotiating abilities (and before I paid close attention to the math), I let clients persuade me to give them "little" 5-percent discounts. On reflection, I probably could have bought a new car with all the $2,500 chunks of money I let slip through my fingers.

## Funny money: No laughing matter

One of the more infamous quotes by a U.S. senator was, "a billion here, a billion there—pretty soon you're talking real money." In fact, the senator summed up the funny-money syndrome pretty accurately. That is to say, if you break down the finances to a level that seems insignificant, the money doesn't actually count. (Isn't it amazing though, how the value of a billion dollars has lost all its meaning to those we elect?)

The funny-money tactic is used on us all the time, and if we're smart, we can either see the tactic for what it is, or turn it around to our advantage).

Think of all the times we've been pitched on term life insurance ("only 14 cents a day") or magazine subscriptions ("only a dollar a week"). These are funny-money tactics. Who, after all, couldn't support a starving child in Bangladesh for only pennies a day?

Funny money is a great negotiating tool. Let's say you and the other side are $1,500 apart on a one-year contract. The other side cordially asks, "Come on, we're so close. Are we really going to let four dollars a day hang us up?"

To which you're tempted to reply, "No, of course not. Let's just sign the deal."

But instead, you bite your tongue and mull it over. Two minutes later you come back with, "Look, let's not play funny money here. Fifteen hundred bucks is a lot of money to me, and I think my service is worth it. I'm offering a fair price as it is, and I'm afraid I can't accept a reduction of this size."

Funny money is a two-way street, after all. If the other side suggests that four bucks a day should have no meaning to you, then it shouldn't to them, either.

# Everything is *not* negotiable

Contrary to what you might have heard, everything is *not* negotiable.

I found this out the hard way recently when I tried to leverage one bank against the other in trying to secure a home loan. I informed the loan officer I was working with that if I couldn't get the interest rate I wanted, I was willing to walk away and take my business to another bank.

"Go ahead; walk," replied the loan officer. "I've got eight other applications on my desk, waiting for approval. If you can get a better deal somewhere else, be my guest."

*He's got a lot of nerve,* I thought. But I sure respect the way he held the line.

Later, I found out that the loan officer's bank had one of the best ratings in the industry, and was one of the most profitable institutions in the country. Eventually, because of other value-added services offered, the same bank that let me walk became my lender, even though they had a higher rate.

Price, of course, is only one aspect of any sale. If the transaction involves a commodity (such as rice, or soybeans, or crude oil, for example), then price may very well be the predominant issue.

A common issue in any business is pricing. Where do you set the price? Is your business positioned to sell to the first-class, coach or economy market? A higher price might infer a higher level of service and attract qualified buyers; or, a high price may turn off customers who know darn well the price is inflated.

The trickiest issue in regard to pricing is discounting. How do you hold the line when all your competitors are slashing prices? Traditionally, the only way to offset a concern surrounding price is to build *value*. Otherwise, the product or service you provide will be viewed as a commodity.

The way to distinguish your product or service and its value-added dimension is to probe for the needs of the buyer, and the potential benefit of what you're selling. Once the need has been identified (and qualified), you'll be in a position to hold the line, or at least reach an agreement in which both parties feel satisfied. (If you are unable to discover a compelling reason why your product or service warrants the full price you charge, then unfortunately, you may have to settle for whatever you can get.)

The loan officer at my bank, for example, was able to secure my business, even though he charged a higher rate of interest than his competitors. The reason? There were other important factors I considered to be of significant value that led to our settlement, such as the amount of the down payment, the fact that I didn't need a co-signer and so on.

## Four steps to a successful settlement

You can sharpen your negotiating skills by following the four steps leading to a successful settlement.

First, *measure* what the other side wants. Before you begin negotiating, find out exactly what the employer is asking for. I know this sounds rather obvious, but you'd be surprised how often a seller will "give away the store" after hearing the customer ask for a concession that's totally vague.

A plea such as, "Oh come on, you can do better than that!" often results in enormous and needless concessions. Finding out from the customer *exactly* how much better you have to do must occur before any serious discussion can take place.

Second, *qualify* the negotiation. If the prospect isn't sincere (or in a position to buy), or has completely unrealistic expectations, you shouldn't be negotiating at all.

What good does it do to settle for a reduced price with a prospective buyer only to have the buyer admit after an hour of haggling that he's not in a position to place an order until the next fiscal year starts six months down the road? You've, in effect, given away the store before the store has even opened for business. A better approach would have been to find out exactly when the prospect was planning on buying and *then* worked out a price. It's

135

a better policy to wait until the time is right before getting locked into a commitment.

I recently received a $15,000 fee from a company in California for the placement of a job candidate. Three years earlier, when I made my very first marketing call to the same company, the company president told me that he was only willing to pay a flat fee of $1,000!

At that time, I simply let him know that I'd like to have his business, but we were so far apart that it didn't make sense to talk. He understood, I kept calling him and finally, years later, we were able to reach an agreement and put together a deal.

By the same token, you must be reasonably certain that your service will produce satisfactory results before you proceed in the negotiation. If you honestly feel that you can't satisfy your customer's needs, why waste each other's time negotiating?

Not long ago, I conducted a seminar for experienced recruiters. One gentleman stood up during the session and told the group that he felt his company's 30-percent fee policy was a form of price gouging—that any fee over 25 percent was a rip-off. I felt badly for the guy, although I don't agree with his premise. He must really have a tough time facing himself in the mirror each morning, feeling he's going to spend the day cheating his customers. Given the way he feels, I don't suppose it would take too much pressure from a prospective client to get him to lower his fee.

If you feel your product or service is inadequate or overpriced, you might as well make any concessions your customers want, and forget negotiating.

## The search for the hidden agenda

The third step in any negotiation is to *probe* for pertinent information. After you know what the other side is proposing, and they're qualified to negotiate with you, try and gather every bit of information you possibly can.

Let's suppose you're negotiating with a home owner for a kitchen remodeling job. What's been the home owner's previous experience with remodeling jobs or construction? With whom has he worked? How did they operate? What did they charge? Was he happy with the results? Why is he now talking to you? What are his expectations? What special services, considerations or materials are important? Is there likely to be additional work in the near future? Is the home owner clear as to exactly what he wants, or is he flexible when it comes to design? Is price an issue? Are terms an issue? Is time an issue?

In other words, take a careful look at what the other side really wants, and what his benefit needs are. Very often in a negotiation, there exists a critical hidden agenda, which will often prove to be the pivotal point. For example, the home owner in the kitchen remodeling example may want his kitchen to look like or perhaps surpass the recent makeover of a neighbor's kitchen, or the boss' kitchen, or a relative's kitchen—ego or pride are at stake (the *real* benefits of the remodeling).

You never know what secrets may be lurking behind the scenes. A hiring manager once confessed to me that the only reason he was negotiating the fee with me was to help his personnel staff save face. Any concession, no matter how minor, he told me, would appear to be a "victory" for them. Did I help him out? Sure.

## The perception is the reality

Finally, *assess* the situation. There are three basic underlying elements in every negotiation: time, information and the assumption of power. In the context of these elements, you'll be able to assess your position relative to the other side and work toward an agreeable solution.

- *Time.* Ask yourself: What are the time considerations in this negotiation? Is anyone under the pressure of a deadline?
- *Information.* Ask yourself: Do I know enough about the situation and everyone's needs, or am I guessing? And by the way, what does the other side know about my needs? Not too much, I hope.
- *Power.* Ask yourself: Do I have an accurate picture of the relative strength or control factors in the negotiation? Which side can least afford to walk away?

137

Remember that in the case of power, the perception can often become the reality. In September 1938, for example, when Neville Chamberlain "saved the world" by appeasing Hitler, he grossly overestimated the strength of the Nazi war machine. The British Prime Minister's failure to accurately assess military power (an inaccuracy fueled by Nazi propaganda) led to a "negotiated" settlement that gave Hitler the green light to inflict untold death and destruction for another seven years. Clearly, a more intelligent negotiation might have truly saved the world.

Before you strike a deal, ask yourself: How much do you need the customer's business? What are your chances of making him happy with the product or service you provide? What will you gain from making a concession? What will you lose? How much anger or disappointment will result from making a concession, and what effect will it have on your relationship or business personality? Do you actually need to make a concession? And if you do make a concession, what will it be?

If what you're about to do makes you uncomfortable, you can always delay. It's better to put off a questionable deal than to agree to something you'll later regret.

And it goes without saying that you should always hold up your end of the bargain once you've negotiated an agreement. Nothing is more frustrating or disillusioning than an episode of bad-faith negotiating. Some people may do it, but you should always stick to the high road. You'll never be sorry for maintaining an elevated standard of ethics.

## Shut up—It's good for business!

A general rule of thumb is to never make the first concession. Even if the other side says, "Your price is too high," the last thing you want to do is say something like, "Well, I guess I could knock 10 percent off." If you do, there's nothing to prevent the customer from saying, "Thanks, but that's not good enough. I need an even deeper discount for you to make the sale."

Instead of coming up with a number at the first opportunity, you should play it close to the vest. "Maybe you could help me out," you might say. "If my price is too high, what exactly did you have in mind that you think would be fair?"

At this point, you should shut up and listen to what the other side has to say. (Sorry, there's no snazzy business school euphemism for the term *shut up*). Even if you have to wait in silence, that's all right, because silence in this situation is your best friend.

Here's a story that I think illustrates several points. A while back, I was approached by a well-known author to ghost-write a chapter on a fairly technical legal subject for a book he was under contract to write. He called me from New York to ask what I would charge for 3,000 words on a write-for-hire basis.

"Gee, I'm not sure," I said. "Do I have to do any research?"

"No, none at all," He replied. "All the research has already been done by a paralegal."

"So why not have the paralegal write the chapter?" I asked.

"Because paralegals can't write," he said. "You can write."

At that point I knew I had him, because his credibility as a writer was at stake. He dreaded having to breathe life into a boring subject, yet didn't trust a researcher to put sparkle in a book that had his name on the cover. What's more, the deadline was fast approaching and his publisher was turning up the heat. In short, he was in a bind.

"So, how much money will you charge me?" he asked.

"Make me an offer that's fair," I said, and then I shut up.

For the next 10 minutes there was a deafening silence. As I waited for his reply, I ran a few numbers. I figured the project would take a couple of days, max. As to the price, I didn't tell him that I normally pay $100 a day for projects like this. I figured that he'd probably offer me $300, maybe $400. But I wasn't going to make the first move; I was going to put the burden on him.

I could tell he was squirming on the other end of the line, hoping that eventually, the silence would drive me to crack and blurt out a price. But I held my ground.

Finally, after 10 minutes of grinding silence, the author spoke up.

"Well, the best I can do is $850," he said.

I probably could've gotten more, but in truth, $850 was more than twice what I would've settled for, so I saw no reason to take the negotiation any further. After a judicious amount of "reflection," I gave him my answer.

"That would be fine," I said. Funny, though, I could sense his reaction on the other end of the line. *Darn it! I should've offered him less!*

# Negotiating gambits

*Gambits* are the tactics used in order to gain advantage in a negotiating situation. Let's look at a few of the gambits that are commonly used to put us on the defensive.

- The *hot potato* gambit is used to dump someone else's problem on you.

"I'm sorry," the prospect tells you, "but the other accountants we've used only charge $15 an hour."
*Wait a minute,* you think. *That's their problem, not mine.*
"Gee, I'm sorry to hear that," you reply. "Maybe the average tax savings of $14,000 a year I find for my clients isn't worth the extra $25 an hour I charge."

- The *higher authority* gambit implicates a third party who somehow stands in the way of getting what you want.

"I hate to bring this up, but I can't agree to your terms," the purchasing manager tells you. "Our accounting department insists on a six-month refundable guarantee."
*There's no way the accounting department outranks the purchasing manager in these matters,* you think to yourself.
"Well, why don't you just waive the guarantee requirements for this particular order?" you respond. "You have that authority, don't you?"

- The *good guy/bad guy* gambit manufactures a real or imaginary "thug" to bludgeon down your price or extract a concession.

"To tell you the truth, you should be glad you're not sitting across from my boss right now," says the vice president. "He's one tough son of a gun and would tear your proposal to shreds. Why don't you and I just reach an agreement now, at the price I want, and we can keep him out of this?"

*I can't believe it! He's using the old good guy/bad guy routine on me!*

"No, I think I'd prefer to meet with your boss face to face," you reply cheerfully. "Maybe I could learn a few things from him about negotiating."

Look for these gambits and their variations the next time you discuss your price, payment terms and conditions, delivery schedules, guarantees, refunds and quality control issues. Recognizing them will save you a lot of money.

## A hundred percent of something

I can't tell you the number of times I've heard the expression, "50 percent of something is better than 100 percent of nothing."

*Hogwash!*

Fifty percent may be better than the full amount, but only in a collection crisis, when someone is cheating you out of what he or she owes you, and you feel lucky to recoup any part of your loss.

Caving in on a regular basis with such a deep concession can be very dangerous. By accepting less than what your service is worth, you not only lose a lot of money; you're also subconsciously "telegraphing" to the world that you're not a believer in what you do for a living. Eventually, this kind of noncommittal attitude will harm your credibility and weaken your earning potential.

A few years ago, I had a "50 percent of something" experience when I worked for a large search firm that proved to be very painful in the short term, but beneficial in the long.

I had cold-called the vice president of a manufacturing company to talk about my executive search service. After a while, it seemed that we'd established a rapport, and, sensing the time was right, I suggested he interview an extremely talented engineering candidate.

"Bill, your candidate sounds like the sort of person we need," said the vice president. "In fact, we're currently conducting a search. However, we're already using a retained search firm on this assignment."

"So you're pleased with the results you're getting," I replied.

"Well, not exactly. You're probably aware of how difficult it is to find an engineer in our type of industry."

"Indeed I am, and that's exactly why I called you. What should we do?"

"Tell you what," said the vice president. "Why don't you talk to Leo, the other recruiter? Tell him the situation; that you have an ideal candidate I want to interview. Maybe the two of you can split the fee. See what he says, and call me back."

*What could be the harm?* I figured.

# King Solomon's dilemma

Sure enough, Leo was receptive to the idea. It turns out he wasn't getting anywhere on the assignment; the engineers he was looking for were too hard to find.

"How about it, Bill? Let's you and I split the fee fifty-fifty," suggested Leo. "That way, we'll both look good. And besides, 50 percent of something is better than 100 percent of nothing, right?"

"Hmm...I'm not sure," I hesitated. "Let me think about it and call you back."

Now I was really confused. So I went to my manager for advice.

"I'm sorry, Bill," he said, shaking his head. "I can't approve a split deal like this."

"But if we don't take it, we might be walking away from a lot of money," I protested. "And besides, there's no guarantee I can find a position for my engineering candidate anywhere else."

"That's just the risk you'll have to take," my manager said. "You see, the issue here isn't the money. The issue is the value of your service."

"What do you mean?"

"It's like this. You took the initiative to cold-call the employer and present your candidate, right?"

"Right."

"And he'd like to interview your candidate because he's perfect for the job."

"This is true," I said.

"Now, let's suppose you were to arrange the interview and, as a result, the company decided to hire the candidate. Haven't you done everything you're trained to do, and done it well?"

"Sure," I answered proudly.

"So aren't you entitled to 100 percent of the fee, and not a penny less?"

"I guess so."

"Now ask yourself this: What did Leo, the other recruiter, do to earn half your money?"

"Nothing," I muttered.

As I walked back to my desk, I thought about what my manager just told me.

*He's right! Why should I give Leo half my fee, just because he happened to have a contract?*

A few minutes later, I called the vice president.

"I spoke with Leo, as you suggested, and he offered to split the fee with me," I said. "But I've got some disappointing news. I thought it over, and I can't in good conscience give Leo half my fee. I just don't feel it's fair."

"I don't blame you," said the vice president. "Leo shouldn't be rewarded for his failure to find me the right person. Unfortunately, I have to stick with Leo, because we signed an exclusive agreement, but I appreciate your calling me. Let's keep in touch."

"Fine. I'll call you in a few months."

Would you like to know how this story ended? Leo finally placed a marginal candidate with the vice president's company. I stayed in touch with the company, and even made a courtesy call to meet the vice president.

Two years later, the candidate Leo placed was fired, and I was asked by the company to fill the vacant position, which I did, for a full fee. If it hadn't been for my manager, I might have caved in and accepted half of what my service was worth. In the end, though, everyone came out ahead, except, of course, Leo and his marginal candidate.

## The power of the printed word

Contracts, proposals and fee agreements can perform a number of valuable functions. The most obvious is that these documents help prevent misunderstandings and specify the responsibilities of each party.

But more importantly, contracts, proposals and fee agreements give you a vehicle for closing a sale. The printed word not only seems to create instant credibility in the mind of the customer (and helps legitimize your position by virtue of the fact that everything's *written down*), but positions your product or service in such a way as to be accepted. Contract, proposals and fee agreements also act as impersonal buffers, and help diffuse any hard feelings or disagreements, as in, "How in the world did *that* get in the contract? There must be a mistake."

A proposal generally spells out what you can do for the customer and an estimate of the cost, while a contract goes further and stipulates precise payment terms, delivery schedules, and so forth.

One of my favorite tools is what I call a "pre-proposal," a document that's different from a proposal in that it never mentions money. The purpose of a pre-proposal is to verify your understanding of the customer's needs, explain the capabilities of your service, and dump qualifying questions in the lap of the customer.

A written pre-proposal, like a verbal negotiation, is designed to measure, qualify, probe and assess the customer before any action takes place. A well-written pre-proposal will also demonstrate your willingness and ability to satisfy your customer's needs. Assuming both you and the customer can tie up any loose ends brought up in the pre-proposal, you can then proceed to the next level, either the delivery of a proposal or the signing of a contract. If you get hung up in the pre-proposal stage, at least you've avoided committing yourself on a price.

Contracts can be long and weighty, or short and sweet. I prefer the latter, unless you have a flaky customer who needs the riot act read to him in advance. The most efficient documents of agreement are those that clearly state what you're going to do, and ask for an acceptance signature all at the same time. However, if you jam-pack your contract with a lot of details, you may be needlessly painting yourself in a corner, promising to deliver more work than is necessary.

Fee agreements are a glorified version of a price list. When I send a fee agreement to a prospective client, I personalize it with the prospect's name and include a place for a signature. In essence, I've converted a price list into a contract, and I've eliminated an unnecessary or time-consuming step.

## A time to reap—Or a time to weep?

If you're faced with the prospect of making a concession, and the sale is important to you, give some thought as to the various ways you might be able to reach an equitable settlement. Remember that if you give up something, you should always get something *meaningful* in return. Otherwise, you'll weep, rather than reap what you sow. Here are some basic ways to negotiate concessions:

- *Splitting the difference.* Your price is $200, but they want it for $100. Don't cave in and offer to split the difference. Let *them* offer to split the difference. Then you can refuse, and get an even better deal.

A few years back, a prospective client asked for a 90-day guarantee. I told him I was sorry, but my standard guarantee was 30 days.

"Why don't we split the difference?" he asked.

"You mean, make it 60 days? Let me think it over."

A couple of days later I called him back.

"I don't think it's fair to give you a 60-day guarantee," I said. "That's double what I give my other customers."

"Well, maybe we could split the difference again," he suggested.

"You mean, make it 45 days? I can live with that."

See how it works? Splitting the difference isn't always a good deal. And if you offer to split the difference, you're leaving yourself open to further concessions.

- *Tit for tat.* This happens all the time in real estate, and it drives me nuts. You're selling your house for $100,000. They want to try to get it for $95,000, so they offer $92,000. You counter with $98,000, they counter your counter with $94,000, you counter their *counter*-counter with $96,000, and you finally settle for $95,000 (with the microwave thrown in for good measure).

A different approach is to just say *no* to tit for tat. When they offer $92,000 and you counter with $98,000, make that your final offer. If they come back with $94,000, simply say, "You're getting a good deal for $98,000, and I won't consider another counteroffer. Take it or leave it."

- *Nibbling.* This is when the buyer gets a few extra goodies at the last minute. Most of us do this when we buy a new car. We let the car dealer make us squirm in his office for three or four hours. Then, just as the papers are about to be signed, we innocently ask, "Oh, by the way, you *are* going to throw in floor mats and pinstriping, aren't you?" More often than not, the dealer will.

However, the dealer may also diffuse your attempt at nibbling by saying, "You did a great job of negotiating and got a really fair price. In fact, my commission will barely buy me lunch at Wendy's. Please don't ask me for anything else. Fair enough?"

- *Extended terms.* Many buyers appreciate a plan that allows them to spread the payments out over several weeks or months. If you agree to such a deal, make sure you get something in return, such as an additional surcharge, an interest charge or, especially if you've agreed to a discount, a penalty for late payment. The penalty might stipulate a reversion to the original or list price if payment is made after a 10-day grace period has passed.

- *Prompt payment.* This is a coin-flip of the extended terms concept, in which you agree to give the customer a discount for making payment in a timely manner. It's not uncommon to reduce the price anywhere from 1 percent to 10 percent if payment is made in full by the customer within 10 days. Or, if you agree on a fixed price that represents a discount, you can stipulate that the buyer pay you in full upon delivery.

- *Volume discount.* This only applies if the order you're given is of sufficient magnitude to warrant a reduction in price. You should always resist the temptation to offer a volume discount for the *promise* of future purchases, since you have no guarantee the purchases will ever be made.

Mastering these negotiation options will not only help you keep your profits up; they'll help you contain your costs when ordering supplies, leasing space or getting the services you need. In every case, negotiating should be a win-win situation. That is, both sides should profit form the negotiation.

For example, I used the volume discount approach when I started using a researcher. When we first discussed the amount of money she wanted for her services, I was told the fee would be $15 an hour.

"May I make a suggestion?" I asked. "I'd prefer to pay you on a daily, rather than an hourly basis. Would $100 a day be all right with you?"

"Sure," she said.

As it turns out, this type of arrangement was good for both of us. The researcher could count on at least a full day's pay every time we did a project together, and I'd save $20 a day, and probably more, since a conscientious researcher will usually put in extra hours each day to complete an assignment.

A negotiated settlement should fall somewhere between horse thievery and letting the horses out of the barn. If you can get what you need and at the same time make the other side happy, then you've done your job, and will have laid the groundwork for a long-term and profitable business partnership.

———◆———

*By learning a few simple tricks,*
*you can earn the money you're worth.*

*Fig. 12.1: A simple, yet effective contract.*

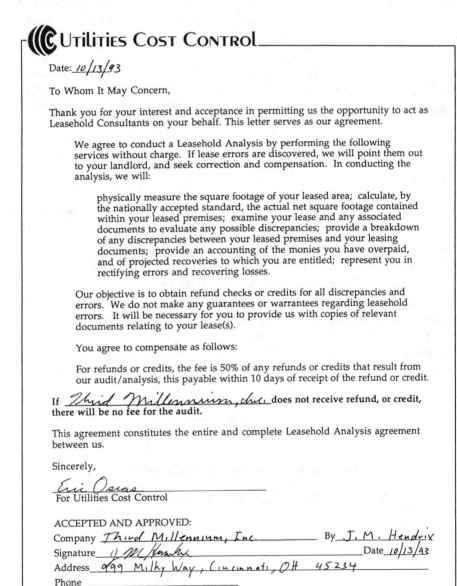

**(C** UTILITIES COST CONTROL

Date: _10/13/93_

To Whom It May Concern,

Thank you for your interest and acceptance in permitting us the opportunity to act as Leasehold Consultants on your behalf. This letter serves as our agreement.

We agree to conduct a Leasehold Analysis by performing the following services without charge. If lease errors are discovered, we will point them out to your landlord, and seek correction and compensation. In conducting the analysis, we will:

physically measure the square footage of your leased area; calculate, by the nationally accepted standard, the actual net square footage contained within your leased premises; examine your lease and any associated documents to evaluate any possible discrepancies; provide a breakdown of any discrepancies between your leased premises and your leasing documents; provide an accounting of the monies you have overpaid, and of projected recoveries to which you are entitled; represent you in rectifying errors and recovering losses.

Our objective is to obtain refund checks or credits for all discrepancies and errors. We do not make any guarantees or warrantees regarding leasehold errors. It will be necessary for you to provide us with copies of relevant documents relating to your lease(s).

You agree to compensate as follows:

For refunds or credits, the fee is 50% of any refunds or credits that result from our audit/analysis, this payable within 10 days of receipt of the refund or credit.

If _Third Millennium, Inc._ does not receive refund, or credit, there will be no fee for the audit.

This agreement constitutes the entire and complete Leasehold Analysis agreement between us.

Sincerely,

_Eric Oscas_
For Utilities Cost Control

ACCEPTED AND APPROVED:
Company _Third Millennium, Inc._ By _J. M. Hendrix_
Signature _J. M. Hendrix_ Date _10/13/93_
Address _899 Milky Way, Cincinnati, OH 45234_
Phone_____

1023 Redway Avenue, Cincinnati, Ohio 45229; 513/751-4266 Fax: 513/221-6288

*Fig. 12.2: This pre-proposal helped define the mission.*

**Radin Associates**
2373 Brother Abdon Way, Santa Fe, NM 87505 • (505) 983-2243 • FAX (505) 983-2244

December 10, 1993

Ms. Randi Lorber, President
INSTRUMENT PRODUCTS, INC.
2900 Gateway Drive
Pompano Beach, FL 33069-4378

Dear Ms. Lorber:

Thanks for spending time with me, and helping me learn more about your organization. I was very impressed with the Instrument Products line of products, and the efficient and up-to-date manner in which they are manufactured.

In regard to the research project we explored, let me play back for you the essence of our discussion, to check my own understanding of your needs.

Instrument Products designs and sells electronic controllers which, simply put, are invaluable in the manufacturing process. However, by virtue of the enormous number of potential applications, many profitable markets are either underexploited or overlooked, due to insufficient name recognition.

Conventional methods of gaining greater industry visibility (such as print advertising, media placement, trade show exhibition, and catalog inclusion) have had a negligible effect in commanding the attention of prospective customers. That's because in a rapidly evolving, highly technical market, it's the *word-of-mouth referrals from centers of influence* that create the greatest impact.

Manfacturers' representatives, therefore, represent the key to greater market penetration, and ultimately, increased sales, since reps are:

• recognized within the engineering community as technical experts;

• regarded by their customers as reasonably objective; and

• positioned by their authority to recommend your company's products.

Ideally, a corps of well-placed manfacturers' reps will act as industry "radio transmitters," broadcasting over a broad band of market frequencies. The trick is how to identify them and stimulate their interest in Instrument Products.

149

*Radin Associates*

2373 Brother Abdon Way. Santa Fe, NM 87505 • (505) 983-2243 • FAX (505) 983-2244

Based on our success with similar projects, Radin Associates will be ideally suited to conduct an exhaustive search for prospective, highly motivated manufacturers' reps. However, in order to produce the best results, we need to answer the following questions:

[1] What is the precise *profile* of the ideal rep firm, in terms of market specialty, customer base, product affiliation, and industry track record?

[2] Which *territories* will yield the greatest return? Do we concentrate in geographic areas that are currently being served by your direct sales force, or do we venture into untested regions?

Once we answer these questions, I can begin the project. Assuming that the project involves the research of a homogeneous geographic area (greater Chicago, for example), the fixed cost will be $7500 for the first location and $5000 for each additional location. Approximately two to three weeks should be allowed for each search.

According to a predetermined schedule, you'll be given a weekly progress report, followed by a complete final report, containing a detailed list of qualified manfacturers' representatives, a recommendation for action, and a compilation of miscellaneous "notes from the trenches."

I will call you on Wednesday, December 12 to discuss the approach we want to take; and I look forward to getting started and successfully completing the work.

Sincerely,

William G. Radin, President
RADIN ASSOCIATES

WGR: gbc

*Fig. 12.3: Nothing beats a follow-on contract!*

## Radin Associates

2373 Brother Abdon Way, Santa Fe, NM 87505 • (505) 983-2243 • FAX (505) 983-2244

March 10, 1994

Ms. Randi Lorber, President
INSTRUMENT PRODUCTS, INC.
2900 Gateway Drive
Pompano Beach, FL 33069-4378

Dear Ms. Lorber:

In response to your request, Radin Associates would be pleased to conduct a research project similar to the one completed on January 25, 1994. The purpose of the new project will be to identify suitable manufacturers' representatives in the Houston metropolitan area.

Upon approval, productive work can begin immediately and will be completed within two weeks, according to the following schedule (assuming a March 29, 1994 start):

| | | |
|---|---|---|
| March 28 | Monday | Begin research, interviewing, networking |
| April 1 | Friday | First written progress report |
| April 8 | Friday | Final written report |

The final written report will include project documentation, a list of qualified referrals, a recommendation for future action, and a compilation of related information which may be of future value to INSTRUMENT PRODUCTS, INC.

The fee for this project will be $5000 plus expenses. Upon receipt of your purchase order, Radin Associates will initiate work on the project. I look forward to working with you.

Sincerely,

3/10/94

William G. Radin, President          Date
RADIN ASSOCIATES

Accepted By:

3-13-94

Randi Lorber, President          Date
INSTRUMENT PRODUCTS, INC.

## Chapter 13

# Breakaway Options: Spin-off, Consulting and Seminar Careers

Now that you've reached that fork in the road, which way should you turn? As we discussed earlier, the career direction you take will need to be based on a number of factors, including your professional interests and abilities, personal needs, income requirements, cash availability, and so on.

In the next four chapters, we'll take a look at 10 of the most common and realistic self-employment options for breakaways: the spin-off solution, the consulting approach, and the seminar trade; the sales free-agency and the MLM crusade; the franchise fraternity and the world of business opportunities; and the high-tech startup, the retail marketplace and the restaurant reality.

As I said in the introduction, my intention is not to steer you toward one career or discourage you from another; I simply want to let you know what you'll be getting into should you decide to pursue a particular dream, and give you a starting point for acquiring more knowledge before you set sail. In the resource section of *Breakaway Careers*, I'll provide you with several reputable sources of additional information on each option, so you can explore the career that strikes your fancy in greater detail.

# 1. The spin-off solution

The most obvious choice when planning your career journey is to go where you've been before, and spin off what you've done at your current or most recent job into your own venture.

The spin-off career makes so much sense because you already have an insight into the field, and the experience to perform whatever you're doing competently. Who's better qualified, for example, than a bar manager at an established upscale restaurant to open a trendy cafe? Or a quality assurance supervisor to start a consulting practice specializing in Total Quality Management?

Undeniably, from a talent and expertise perspective, a spin-off is a logical choice for many breakaways. However, before your maiden voyage, it would be best to check your career ship for leaks.

## It takes more than knowledge

Assuming you possess an adequate knowledge of your field, you should try to avoid these attitudinal and strategic problems that may cause your business to founder:

- *Overconfidence.* Just because you've been a whiz kid working for someone else doesn't necessarily mean you'll succeed as a business owner. By keeping a watchful eye on the daily details, you'll make sure the terms *bright* and *broke* aren't mutually exclusive.

- *Oversaturation.* You may want to start a competing office supply store down the street from where you used to work; but check first to see if the market can support another store in the same territory with a generally equal level of inventory and service.

- *Overfamiliarity.* Remember the old saying, "Familiarity breeds contempt"? Make sure you're not too burned out on what you've spent the last few years doing. In the long haul, it'll take more than simply a change of venue to fuel your interest in the trade.

- *Overimpatience.* As with any endeavor, it'll take an adequate amount of time to get things rolling. Many people who spin off expect there to be little interruption in business activity, when in fact, success may simply come to those who wait.

- *Overdependence.* If you rely too heavily on one set of customers (or people who simply *promised* you their patronage), you may be headed for trouble. Put your eggs in several baskets to avoid the "mother hen" syndrome.

- *Overdeveloped self-reliance.* There are a lot of truly knowledgeable people out there who can really help you improve your business, and nothing turns them off more than a "know-it-all." A case in point: I have a good friend who's totally self-taught in everything he does, and he's incapable of learning from anyone else. As a result, well-meaning people in a position to teach him things have given up trying. While self-reliance can be a virtue, there's a limit to how much you can learn without third-party instruction.

- *Overwhelming information.* This is the opposite of self-reliance, in which information overload creates paralysis. The self-employed are besieged daily by purveyors of new computer hardware and software, long-distance services, newsletters, office supply catalogs, directories, and so forth. If you're not careful, you'll make a career out of sorting through information that adds nothing to your bottom line.

In addition, you should beware of giving too much credence to personal and professional acquaintances who want to load you up with their opinions and helpful hints. Although there may be value buried in their advice, at some point you'll need to make timely decisions based on your own instincts and business acumen. Otherwise, you'll be pulled in a million different directions.

# Restrictive covenants

Of increasing concern to anyone starting a business in our litigious culture is the chance, no matter how remote, that a spin-off endeavor might in some way be perceived as a breach of ethics or confidentiality in the eyes of a past employer.

A growing number of companies, particularly in the high-tech fields, are beginning to bind their employees to noncompete agreements, either by implication or written contract. Such *restrictive covenants* represent an attempt by employers to prevent people who might have access to proprietary information from "stealing" company blueprints, software, customer lists, formulas or any other types of trade secrets or "intellectual property" when they change jobs or spin off their own businesses.

As you can imagine, terms like trade secrets and intellectual property are somewhat nebulous, and can have about as many interpretations as the terms "family values" or "resisting arrest." Depending on your point of view (and what's at stake), a trade secret or intellectual property can be anything from an innovative scientific breakthrough in biotech engineering to the combination of your manager's locker at the company health club.

Noncompete agreements vary considerably in the restrictions they seek to impose, but usually they focus on the issues of time, location and market. For example, if you've worked for a high-tech automotive electronics supplier in Detroit, your noncompete clause may prevent you from starting a company that sells competing products based on similar technology in the Detroit metropolitan area for a period of two years.

# Making a graceful exit

Although many noncompete claims that find their way into the courts are frivolous and without merit, it's a good idea to carefully review any employment documents you may have signed while working for a past employer.

If you feel you might be vulnerable to a lawsuit or injunction, check with your attorney for clarification of any documents you may have signed, to weigh the risks involved. Make sure your attorney is knowledgeable about employment as it pertains to protecting the rights of the employee. In hindsight, I realized that the attorney I consulted with in regard to my own situation worked for a large law firm whose attorneys worked exclusively on the behalf of the employer. All they knew was how to sue employees, rather than protect their rights!

In all likelihood, I never would have been slapped with a suit or injunction had I challenged the restrictive covenants of the company. Of course, if I had, guess who'd have the advantage in a court of law—the newly indigent renegade employee; or the $400 million corporation?

Lest you needlessly raise the hackles of a former employer, here are some simple precautions to take that will minimize the risk of problems after your departure:

1. At the time of your resignation, be sure to surrender all company property in your possession, such as a company vehicle, office keys, ID badges, computer hardware and/or software, demonstration materials, contracts, files or credit cards.

2. Ask your supervisor to designate a *responsible company official* to oversee your exit, and to accompany you whenever you're "on site" in the future.

Since a noncompete clause (either valid or frivolous) can gum up your breakaway career, check with your attorney before you start your spin-off. It's best to keep your bases covered.

## To write every wrong

For all you know, the enforcement of a noncompete agreement can have a serendipitous effect. In an odd twist of fate, I would never have become an author had it not been for the fact that I was legally barred (at least, so I thought) from my chosen profession the day I became a breakaway.

After I quit my management job, I was faced with the realization that my employment contract expressly forbade me from engaging in the practice of executive search for a period of six months. Frustrated, I broached the subject of exactly what I could and couldn't do with the company president shortly after my departure, to see if I could work out a compromise.

"Let me see if I understand the conditions of my contract," I began. "I can't work within a 50-mile radius of my home as a headhunter for half a year, right?"

"That's right," said my former boss.

"And that's because the corporation feels I may use proprietary information gathered here at my job that may be injurious to my former employer, right?"

"That's right," he said.

"So if I can't work as a headhunter, is there any reason I can't work as a *trainer,* helping other headhunters to improve their skills?" I asked.

"I don't see why not."

"Good," I said. "Then that's what I'll do. I'll be a headhunter trainer."

Later that same day at home, I lugged a foot-high stack of training materials I'd gathered over the years out of the closet and dumped them on all my desk. *Whoomp!*

*What do I do now?* I asked myself as I puzzled over several hundred pages of miscellaneous notes, statistics, questionnaires and handouts. It was obvious there was a wealth of information scattered about my desk, but it was in serious need of, well, structure. Suddenly I had a brainstorm.

*I know! I'll write a book. It'll help me organize my thoughts and give me the credibility I need to solicit business as a trainer.*

## What color is your lemonade?

My decision was that spontaneous. If I could just break even on the book, I figured the whole writing exercise would be worthwhile. It didn't even faze me that I'd never written anything other than an occasional (and undistinguished) term paper on such subjects as Haydn and Mozart many years earlier in music school.

*So what?* I thought. *I'll just teach myself whatever I need to learn about how to write, self-publish and market a nonfiction paperback book.*

As it turns out, I never had so much fun as I did with *Billing Power! The Recruiter's Guide to Peak Performance*. And the more I wrote, the more I enjoyed it. Ironically, the legal restriction against spinning off a search firm had spawned an entirely new career. Lemons into lemonade, so to speak.

# 2. The consulting approach

It used to be said that a consultant was merely a person paid a lot of money to look at your watch and tell you what time it was. And in some circles, the term "consultant" still has negative overtones, in that it describes someone who's either collecting a fee for reporting what's obvious, or is simply unemployed and can't find a job.

These, however, are boom times for consultants, especially in the era of the "shamrock organization," a term coined by Charles Handy, a professor at the London School of Business and author of *The Age of Unreason*. Handy, himself a well-known consultant to business, has chronicled the recent proliferation of organizations who are run by a core of key executives, who in turn are supported by consultants, contractors and part-time workers.

Look around you at big companies like IBM, General Electric and Procter & Gamble. There're all downsizing, and either "temping out" or subcontracting work that was formerly the domain of the salaried employee with benefits. In fact, the identity of the largest employer in America may surprise you: Manpower, Inc., a worldwide temporary personnel services organization with more than 900 local offices nationwide.

## Consulting in the shamrock era

The point is, as corporations continue to shed more and more layers of "captive" employees, there will be an increasing demand for independent work providers—many of them consultants. Here are a few of the areas in which a typical company might turn to consultants as an outsourcing solution:

- *Special projects.* The Yucca Fertilizer Company wants to change its image with its neighbors in the Albuquerque area. So the company hires Marcia Wolf, a public relations consultant, to generate favorable press reports, update the corporate logo and perhaps find a more pleasant-sounding name.

- *Ongoing functions.* Since it began downsizing a few years back, Yucca no longer employs a full-time corporate communications director. However, it "downloads" the publication of its monthly employee newsletter to Pat Codd, an experienced freelance editor with a desktop publishing capability.

- *Information gathering.* To keep abreast of the constant stream of new regulations and pending legislation affecting the fertilizer industry, Yucca relies on Lynn Sontag, a freelance *infopreneur* to comb through libraries and access databases where the relevant red tape resides. The marketing department also uses Lynn's considerable research skills whenever issues such as pricing, trade name restrictions or consumer preferences reach the corporate front burner.

- *Interim executive positions.* Yucca, in an effort to improve its cash flow, has decided to shut down its sister division, King Cattle Enterprises. So it hires retired livestock executives Eli Velarde and Lorenzo Sanchez on a six-month consulting contract to oversee the plant closure.

- *Cost reduction/refund services.* Convinced that the company is being overcharged on its shipping costs, Yucca hires Sander Nassan, a cost reduction consultant, to examine freight invoices from the past three years. Sander will then recommend ways to reduce future costs and negotiate a refund for past overpayment.

In addition to the services that are already supplied by consultants, Yucca also plans to outsource its data processing, product testing, payroll and employee relocation functions to third-party organizations.

# Anything for a Buck

To provide effective consulting services, it's not always necessary to be a world-renowned authority on any given subject, especially with the availability of information resources (and other
consultants you can subcontract with) at your disposal.

Chuck Weideman, my mentor at SCORE, worked for more
than 40 years with an international consulting firm before he retired. A true believer in his firm's immortal tongue-in-cheek motto
("Anything for a Buck"), Chuck's advice to me was to seek out new
consulting opportunities, even if I was something less than an
expert on the *topic du jour.*

As it turns out, his advice was duly noted and, in 1993, I billed
more than $25,000 for consulting work for which I was only mar-
ginally prepared to accept, but which I completed to the client's
satisfaction.

# Training the consultants: Truth or consequences?

Many franchised and nonfranchised consulting practices are
now available, in which you can receive invaluable technical training from the parent organization, sponsor, licenser or business
opportunity trainer, either by way of seminars or correspondence
courses. The trick to becoming a consultant in a new field is to
make sure you don't get in over your head; or fall prey to a con
game in which half-truths are passed off as reality by the experts
who want to exchange their training for your greenbacks.

For example, a common scam of some consulting business
opportunities that offer "training" is to lead you to believe that you
can quickly acquire the technical proficiency needed to satisfy your
customers, with ongoing technical support offered freely by the
people who originally trained you.

What they don't tell you is that the information you need to
satisfy your customers' needs might in fact be beyond your ability
or inclination to master, and that you may end up spending all
your time groping for answers while your business development
activities take a back seat.

The result of these scams is that the trainers ultimately offer
to take over the technical part of your business (for which they

receive compensation), leaving you at their mercy, without the very income stream that's crucial to your success.

While many organizations offer honest, practical training that can quickly be translated into profits, beware of any outfit that paints a simplistic picture of the technical nuances required to perform their particular brand of consulting. Unless you know the truth, you may be forced to deal with the consequences.

## The breakaway and consumer markets

Small businesses and individuals are also in need of consultants. Without the help of freelance computer whiz Bill Gwynne, for example, I'd be in a state of perpetual crisis (or at the very least, anxiety) when it comes to my Macintosh needs.

Any time I need to evaluate new equipment, install software or troubleshoot those maddening glitches, crashes and system failures, I can count on Bill to hold my hand or point me in the right direction. I figure he's saved me thousands of dollars (and untold aggravation) over the years, and since I'm a borderline computer phobic, nothing beats the sense of security knowing Bill's just a phone call away.

Consultants can serve anyone who's in need of help. In the new-age town where I live, there are consumer-oriented consultants that deal with every imaginable issue, from your image, your career, your home remodeling, your interpersonal conflicts and your finances to your diet, your pet loss grieving and your reincarnation possibilities.

## Calculating fees

The most common dollars-and-cents mistake you can make as a consultant is to undercharge for your services. Remember, the cost of getting business and doing business should be factored into your fees, otherwise you'll never make a profit. For example, it can take several hours to adequately write a proposal, so factor the time you spent writing it and negotiating your contract with the client into your fee.

Fees can be charged on a flat rate (usually per project), a sliding scale, a long-term retained rate (per the terms of your contract, and paid on a monthly basis), an hourly rate, or on a cost-plus basis (a base, or fixed fee plus any cost overruns). For new clients, it's advisable to get an advance or a guarantee and, by all means, make sure you get reimbursed for all approved expenses, including long-distance charges, fax, photocopying, postage, overnight delivery, travel and meals. Or, ask for a daily *per diem* to cover your estimated out-of-pocket expenses.

Don't overlook the consulting opportunities that can be performed over the telephone. By accepting credit cards or setting up a 900 number, you can make it easy for customers anywhere in the world to benefit from your expertise.

## 3. The seminar trade

A natural extension of the consulting business is the seminar trade, in which you impart your knowledge face-to-face with those willing to pay for it by giving speeches, presentations, workshops or training sessions.

There are two basic avenues to seminar success, depending on the degree of risk you're willing to assume:

1. *Self-sponsored seminars* are those in which you to incur your own promotion, travel and site rental expenses. Depending on the success of your promotion, the seminar you give at the Secaucus, New Jersey, Holiday Inn entitled, "How to Raise Llamas for Fun and Profit" may attract enough people to earn you a huge profit. Or it may not.

2. *In-house seminars* are those underwritten or sponsored by a particular organization whose membership, presumably, will be interested in your talk. In-house seminars can be given at the sponsor's site (as in a church or company auditorium), or off-site at a local hotel or banquet room.

Despite the fact that there is no guaranteed wage, many speakers prefer the increased control and generally greater earning potential of the self-sponsored seminar. In addition, there are some topics, such as in the self-help and recovery fields, that don't easily lend themselves to outside sponsorship.

The advantage of the in-house seminar is that you can concentrate more on your topic and worry less about the promotional aspects. And if your audience likes your presentation, you'll be asked to return at a later date, or address similar or related organizations. Before you know it, you'll be on the "circuit," hopping from one cat show (or human resource managers trade meeting, or weight loss symposium or antique fair) to the next.

## Seminar topics

Speech or seminar topics can vary widely, of course; and can provide the audience with everything from down-home entertainment to business management training to self-improvement, motivational or investment strategies. They can be political in nature (Anita Hill makes a reported $12,000 per appearance), or simply give the participants a short-lived feel-good experience (known in the trade as a *warm bath*).

One of the most interesting seminars I ever attended was one in which the seminar leader psyched those of us in attendance into walking barefoot over a 14-foot-long bed of burning coals. Now *that* was invigorating.

Whether your goal is to provide hard-core, tangible information to the participants or just warm up the crowd for the main act (known as a *keynote*), your ultimate objective as a professional speaker should be the same: making money.

Unless ego gratification is your only motive, it makes no sense to spend the effort traveling around the country just to break even. Generally speaking, the more useful the content, the more you get asked to speak, and the more revenue you generate. Even celebrity speakers suffer if their content is weak or uninteresting, and leaves the audience with little to cling to in the way of inspiration, new ideas or a call to action.

If your subject matter is meant to help other people, make sure you give the audience tangible information they can take home with them. If they can't take several pages of notes, for example, during a four-hour presentation, then your content is either weak or disorganized.

## Forget Toastmasters, this is a business

While it might seem that only those individuals blessed with a silver tongue can make a living as a public speaker, remember, the key to success goes beyond oratorical prowess; it lies in three basic areas: marketing, content and back-of-the-room sales.

Professional public speaking has little to do with a biweekly meeting with the local chapter of Toastmasters, in which the ultimate goal is to deliver a three-minute speech. Public speaking is a down-and-dirty, grind-'em-out exercise in marketing strategy and physical stamina, in which long hours, connecting flights and hotel food are the standard bill of fare.

There are several ways to market your seminar. Direct mail, telemarketing and display advertising tend to work well when promoting your own self-sponsored presentation. For targeting specific organizations for in-house seminars, the better your list of contacts, the better your chance of pitching your seminar.

You should always have adequate support materials once you get your foot in the door with a potential sponsor. Brochures, reviews, testimonials and a list of topics (with a brief description of each one) should be prepared to build the case as to the benefits of your seminar, and how it will improve the lives of those in attendance.

You should constantly revise and/or add to your list of topics, to avoid your presentation getting stale. At the very least, you should periodically re-title your topics to give them a current-sounding edge. The old joke in the seminar trade revolves around the speaker who's got one speech with 37 different titles, giving the sponsors a wide selection of choices.

## Books, reports and videotapes

When I set out to train other headhunters, I figured that having written a book on the subject of recruiting would add to my credibility, and therefore my ability to book more business. And I was right.

What never crossed my mind was the income-generating potential of the book in terms of back-of-the-room sales—but I caught on very quickly.

In fact, it wasn't long before I realized that the profits in any given seminar lie not behind the podium, but near the rear door. Based on my own experiences and those of other trainers, I came to the conclusion that the more skillful the speaker, the more *product* the audience will want to purchase. First-rate professional speakers earn far more money selling product than they do from their speaking fees; so naturally, a big part of their success is tied to the quality and quantity of the products they make available for purchase during the breaks and after the presentation. And this is true in all venues, including in-house seminars with only a dozen participants in attendance.

Suddenly, I found myself selling dozens of books every time I spoke. At $39.95 a book, it wasn't unusual to rack up several thousand dollars per seminar. And I only consider myself to be an average speaker. Really good speakers can sell up to $10,000 or $20,000 a day worth of books, audio cassettes, videotapes, abstracts, booklets, newsletters, in-house consulting services, and so forth. They set up attractive displays near the entrance of the hall, and they hire an assistant to handle the purchasing transactions. They also make sure to get a complete attendee list from the sponsor or have the attendees sign up for a giveaway, in order to build a prospect list for future use.

Once I realized the income potential that came from the back of the room, I wrote a second book, *The Recruiter's Almanac* ($49.95), and developed a set of booklets I called the *Career Development Reports* to offer the seminar attendees more ways to take me home with them.

Sure, it's a hassle to lug a suitcase full of books through the Canton/Akron airport; but it sure feels nice the next day when the suitcase is empty and my briefcase is stuffed with checks and credit card carbons.

As in consulting, you should require that the sponsor of your in-house seminar reimburse you for your expenses, especially travel and meals. In terms of fees, you should charge an amount that's proportional to the number of hours you need to invest in preparing your subject matter, or the price the sponsor is willing to pay, whichever is higher.

Of greater importance is the purchasing power of the audience, in terms of size, affluence and tendency. Back-of-the-room potential should always be a key factor in the pricing of your seminar, whether you're setting the price with the sponsors of an in-house seminar or the *registration fee* for a self-sponsored affair.

Figure in the *hassle quotient* every time you consider doing a speech. Is $250 a reasonable fee for a half-hour talk? Sure, if it's in your hometown on a weeknight and there are 100 attendees. On the other hand, if the sponsors expect you to travel 400 miles by air at your own expense to talk to a group of 14 people, then it's not worth the hassle.

As long as you can offer information that's of value to your constituency...

◆

*You can find a way to profit from spin-off, consulting and seminar careers.*

# Chapter 14

# Breakaway Options: Rep, Distributor and MLM Opportunities

If you're the type of person who thrives on meeting different people every day, and you enjoy getting results from your own efforts, then a career in independent selling might very well be for you.

Unlike the standard sales career progression with a company, in which your sales achievements are rewarded by increased managerial and administrative responsibilities, an independent selling career will enable you to do what you like best—selling—without the intrusions and headaches of dealing with a bureaucracy.

As it turns out, many manufacturers or product originators (known as *principals*) prefer not to employ direct salespeople in the field, but to organize an independent sales force made up of manufacturers' representatives (or *agents*), distributors, value-added resellers (VARs) or value-added distributors (VADs).

It's not uncommon these days for principals to mix and match different sales channels, depending on the type of product or service being sold, or the demographics of the territories being covered.

Several of my consulting clients, for example, who are manufacturers of sophisticated computer-based instrumentation, employ direct field salespeople in some geographic territories, and manufacturers' reps in the rest. Other manufacturers I know sell exclusively through distributors, while employing regional sales managers to train and oversee the activities of the distributors in their respective jurisdictions.

# Understanding rep economics

Needless to say, the outsourcing trend in the sales force is thoroughly consistent with the shamrock organizational paradigm that's so much in vogue these days. And without a doubt, the reason more and more companies are selling through independent channels (a fact that only increases your opportunities and potential value to principals) boils down to simple economics.

It costs somewhere in the neighborhood of $75,000 to $100,000 per year in base salary, training, reimbursed travel and benefits to keep a direct salesperson employed in any given territory. Therefore, if the salesperson in that territory generates less revenue than that, then the company loses money.

On the other hand, by entering into a contract with an independent rep or distributor, the principal can minimize its loss potential. Since it costs only a fraction of the dollar amount invested in a direct employee to sign up and maintain a relationship with a rep or distributor, practically everything the rep sells can be added to the company's bottom line. In other words, no risk, all gain.

Principals also like reps because they presumably have a knowledge of the product (otherwise they wouldn't be signed up), a work ethic (there's no cushy salary to fall back on), a high degree of motivation (most self-employed reps are in their mid 40s when they go into business, and more than likely have greater financial responsibilities than someone half their age), and consistency in the field (many independent reps are in it for the long haul, and quite a few bring their progeny into the business with them).

# 4. Reps and distributors

Before you seriously consider the life of independent selling, let's define the legal distinctions between reps and distributors, since the lines are often blurry. Reps and distributors both act as sales agents of their principals, but reps, unlike distributors, do not take title to the product. That is, they don't purchase the product for resale to their customers.

Since distributors actually own what they sell, they can set prices however they want after they purchase the product at wholesale or cost, and can often make more of a gross profit. That is, they can buy a $100 item from the manufacturer at $50 and sell it back to the customer for $100. However, distributors must raise the cash to buy the product, assume the costs of carrying the inventory, and risk their investment by offering to their customers a product that may not sell. So while a distributor's gross may be higher than that of a rep, their net may in fact be less.

## Commissions, territories and perceived value

Reps, on the other hand, keep no purchased inventory on hand, and work with the principal on a commission-only (or *straight commission*) basis. They either receive payment when they turn in an order (which is charged back against future commissions should the deal go south), or upon receipt of the customer's check to the principal upon delivery. In most cases, commission checks are cut on a monthly basis.

Commissions will vary from one product category to the next, and within each category. Commissions on pharmaceutical products, for example, range from 7 percent to 12 percent; while commissions on sports goods and supplies generally fall in the 4-percent to 9-percent range. To find out if a specific commission schedule is reasonable and customary, compare what two or three different manufacturers are offering for the sale of similar products; or consult a published commission survey in the industry you wish to represent.

Another distinction between reps and distributors centers around the issue of territories. Any respectable rep agreement will

169

specify a highly defined geographic territory that's yours and yours alone. The territory may be as small as a zip code or as large as a contiguous five-state region, but it will always be granted to you on an exclusive basis.

In contrast, distributors are generally placed in an every-man-for-himself position with the principal. It's not uncommon, for example, for a manufacturer to have several distributors in the same town; and even though some principals go through the charade of mapping out restricted geographic boundaries for each of their distributors, these types of territorial restrictions are pretty much unenforceable. Besides, from the principal's perspective, if the customers in a given city with five "restricted" territories want to engage in a feeding frenzy over the product, who cares about the distributors' territories, anyway?

In the high-tech world, where *solutions* are just as important as products, the term "value-added" has become a popular prefix that frequently appears alongside the title of distributor or reseller. To earn the status of value-added reseller, you must possess a technical expertise of sufficient depth to enable you to "objectify" your customer's needs in a credible fashion and provide overall guidance on a wide variety of needs affecting a total system, not just a particular product.

In essence, a VAR is a distributor who buys goods wholesale and enhances them before reselling them to the end-user. In the computer world, for example, the enhancement may take the form of peripherals and/or software added to a basic CPU, keyboard and color monitor. If the VAR is truly an expert in the field, then he or she will continually be searching for new combinations or customizations of products to meet the customer's requirements.

Additional enhancements by a VAR may include training and on-the-phone technical support. If the VAR handles more than one principal, then the value to the end-user is greatly increased, since the VAR can more honestly seek the best solution, rather than use his or her position with the customer to (as they say) *push iron.*

## Rep markets and selling cycles

Practically any product or service can be sold on an independent basis. Since there are no startup inventory costs as a rep,

170

all you need is the desire to get out in the field and start making sales calls. Since you're acting merely as the sales channel for the principal, you need not concern yourself directly with issues such as advertising, product quality, liability or customer service. Your job is to move product.

As a rep, you'll be selling into one of three markets: *business to business, industrial* and *consumer.* The business-to-business market is often referred to as the *OEM* market, in that you'll be selling to *original equipment manufacturers,* or those who make component parts specifically for use in the products (or original equipment) of manufacturers who put their brand names on the label.

For example, a customized valve that's sold to a motor manufacturer is an OEM product when the valve is merely a part of a motor that's sold under the motor manufacturer's trademark.

The same valve, however, would be considered an industrial product if it were sold to a pulp and paper plant, where it would be used exclusively on in-house factory equipment.

Consumer products, such as clothing, accessories, gifts and toys, are never sold directly by reps to consumers, only to retailers, wholesalers and distributors who, in some cases, may sell to end-users.

As you might expect, the selling cycle and complexity of the sale will vary considerably from one product to the next. Landing a big electronic component order (or *program*) with an aerospace customer will take a significantly longer amount of time to put together than the sale of three dozen novelty items to a local drugstore.

It stands to reason, then, that when you're estimating how long it will take you to become profitable, you'll need to consider the sales volume and buying frequency of your target market.

## Getting started as an independent rep

If you're interested in selling a particular manufacturer's product, you can contact the manufacturer directly at the corporate office. As a general rule, it'll be next to impossible to pry a principal away from an existing rep, especially if you're just starting out. However, if the principal is unhappy with the incumbent rep, they may already be in the process of recruiting and interviewing prospective reps. In such a case, you might be well-positioned to pick up a company's line of products.

An excellent source of current opportunities for reps can be found in *Agency Sales Magazine*, a monthly publication of the Manufacturers' Agents National Association (MANA), a trade organization serving the interests of more than 11,000 reps nationwide. In addition to its articles offering useful advice on growing your rep business, *Agency Sales* also features a large classified ad section for its readers, in which reps can solicit for lines, and principals can solicit for reps.

Most reps carry from eight to 12 lines at a time. The natural tendency is to milk the two or three really "hot" lines that are generating the most sales activity. However, this approach can lead to trouble, in that the lion's share of your business becomes overly dependent on the success of a particular product. By putting all your eggs in one basket, you also run the risk of angering your neglected principals, a practice that might lead to having some of your lines taken away from you.

Once you get the business rolling, you might find yourself faced with the following predicament, namely: What do you do if you find your territory saturated or too overwhelming to adequately service? Do you add more lines or hire additional salespeople?

"That's an easy question to answer," says Bert Holtje, editor of *Agency Sales* and president of James Peter Associates, a rep firm in Tenafly, New Jersey.

"Lines aren't expanded, territories are. The smart agent will hire more sales people to get better coverage. Once you start adding too many lines, you're headed for trouble."

## Building a partnership with the principal

Aside from having decent lines and a geographic territory with solid customer potential, nothing is more important to a rep than a partnership with the principal, which begins with the signing of a mutually beneficial contract.

Even though the rep business has historically been conducted in an honest fashion, it's in your best interest for both sides to be clear on issues such as territories, commissions, payment schedules, termination of contract, and so forth. If the principal resists signing a contract, it probably says something about the way the company plans to do business. As Yogi Berra once said, "A verbal contract isn't worth the paper it's written on."

Once a contract is signed, there are a number of critical issues that define the rep/principal relationship.

These include:

- *Product quality.* If your customers don't think much of what you're selling, then it'll be hard to sustain a good relationship with the manufacturer. If this is the case, do your principal a favor, and explain how your customers feel. If they take the complaints to heart, fine. If they don't, find another principal.

- *Training.* Highly engineered products usually require some initial and ongoing training on the part of the rep. If you can't explain the newest features (much less the operation) of a particular product, your credibility with the customer is likely to be shot, along with your sales dollars.

- *Responsiveness.* Nothing frosts a rep more than having to wait three weeks for a quote or a delivery commitment from a principal. Delays not only tend to lose sales (and income); they also result in a loss of face for the rep, who looks like a fool when pleading to get a manufacturer to take action.

- *Communication.* On occasion, a delivery or quality problem with the product will cause friction with the customer—friction that could have been avoided with a simple phone call or fax from the principal.

- *Lead generosity.* Customers often make calls directly to the manufacturer asking for product or price information. By contract, it's the principal's responsibility to turn over leads to the rep who covers the customer's territory. Lead hoarding by the principal results in unfilled orders and (justifiable) anger by the rep. In a worst-case scenario, customer inquiries are filled directly at the corporate office, which is usually illegal and in violation of the trust the rep places in the manufacturer.

- *Line generosity.* Reps depend on their lines to make their living. When a principal yanks a line out from under a rep without notice, it generally hurts both parties. If the principal is in some way dissatisfied with your performance, then they owe it to you to make their displeasure known.

- *Territorial generosity.* Reps respond well to a principal's vote of confidence. Unless you're really underachieving in a given territory, there's no reason for the principal to split your territory or assign some of your customers to another rep, or (worse yet), expropriate them as "house accounts." Your contract should protect you from these practices; if it doesn't, you probably need a new contract.

- *Autonomy in negotiation.* It's the principal's right to enter into negotiations directly with the customer when a large order is under discussion. That's because they're in the best position to understand the profit or loss that's at stake. However, it's incumbent upon them to keep you in the loop, since your input can be valuable during the negotiations, and the act of cutting you out makes you look impotent to the customer, someone whose respect you've been cultivating for quite some time.

There is, of course, an occupational hazard connected to the rep business. If your revenues soar in a given territory, there's a good chance your principal will take the line away from you and assign a direct employee to cover your territory.

Most industry experts consider this maneuver, which is based on simplistic economics, to be greedy (and foolish), since it's the rep who brought in the business in the first place and is presumably perpetuating the product's sales. Replacing a rep who's spent years building the customer's trust with a direct employee sends a very bad signal to the customer.

However, this tactic is commonplace in the industry, so it's best to keep a nice balance among all your lines (and stay on the lookout for new ones to add). Just don't be surprised if, by successfully building up a territory, you've worked yourself out of a job.

# 5. MLM: A different kind of distributorship

The concept of getting the product directly under the nose of the customer without the expense of advertising or conventional retailing naturally has a great deal of appeal to manufacturers. Recently, more and more companies have begun to exploit a rather unconventional strategy called multi-level marketing (or MLM), whose objective is to put the sales team on the front line as entrepreneurs, giving them a vehicle to earn unlimited income through the sale of product.

In a nutshell, here's how multi-level marketing works:

- You and the parent company sign a distributorship agreement, in which you, as an independent contractor, are licensed to sell the company's product in a nonexclusive territory.

- You purchase a starter kit that includes training materials, company sales literature and a supply of product to sell.

- By agreement, you're entitled to charge a markup on the products you sell, with the ability to purchase freely as much product as you need for resale. The markup amount is yours to keep.

- You're also encouraged to sign up new distributors, who are given the same deal as you, only you now receive an override, or commission on a portion of the sales revenues generated by your recruits, that is, those you now "manage."

- It's understood that the potential for earnings from the overrides far exceeds the amount you could ever earn from your own individual sales efforts.

- Your goal, then, is to develop a *downline* of distributors from which a stream of overrides flows.

175

- Your direct recruits are each encouraged to recruit their own new distributors, enabling them to develop their downlines, making them only slightly less rich than you.

- The company, with minimal effort, reaps the rewards of having untold thousands of distributors, each buying starter kits, selling product, and recruiting even more distributors.

If this whole *shtick* sounds like a pyramid scheme, that's because it is. Those at the top of the pyramid are rewarded exponentially for the work done further down the chain. In fact, they're dependent on their individual downlines to keep the money flowing in. Those further down the chain must have faith that they, too, will develop similar downlines of their own.

A downline is like a giant river that needs to reach a certain volume before it can generate a sizable cash flow. Constant replenishment and the formation of new tributaries will guarantee a steady stream of residual income. In the absence of new recruits or a stable sales force, however, the chain will eventually break and the source of income will dry up.

## Income supplement or a full-blown career?

Multi-level marketing represents an innovative (and brilliant) approach to bringing product to market. Companies such as Mary Kay Cosmetics, Amway and NuSkin have made many of their distributors (as well as their executives) fabulously wealthy from this nontraditional method of marketing. Most often, consumer products such as cosmetics, cleansers, books, toys and car care supplies are the standard fare of MLM organizations. However, intangible products such as life insurance and long-distance services are also sold via the MLM approach.

Multi-level marketing can be viewed simply as a way to supplement your income by selling moderate amounts of product in your spare time, or as a vehicle to financial independence (which is the way it's usually presented to potential recruits). Generally, there are minimum sales quotas for distributors. However, the ultimate goal of any MLM scheme is to make millionaires out of the select few who approach the game with a high level of dedication, loyalty and missionary fervor.

## The distinctions make the difference

As you can imagine, there are plenty of scam operations that pose as legitimate MLM opportunities. If you're seriously evaluating a distributorship, be sure to look for these key differences:

- *Initiation rites.* It you're required to load up with a ton of inventory and buy into a whole bunch of training materials, then you might be in for trouble. Sure, it's only natural for companies to want to make it worth their while to bring new recruits up to speed. But theoretically, their money should be made through the sale of product to consumers, not through the gang-tackling of new distributors. If you're asked to invest more than a couple of hundred dollars in the program, you might think twice about your role in the company's revenue generation plans.
- *Recruiting violations.* If the company's main concern centers around recruiting, they might be crossing the line between using the MLM method to sell product and the MLM method to build a pyramid scheme around a phantom product, one that's used simply as a front to make the upline rich.

MLM organizations such as NuSkin have come under attack from government agencies and investigative reporters for crossing the line in both initiation and recruiting. The problem is, the line is very difficult to define from a legal perspective.

## Downline or downside?

I was recruited into the NuSkin organization a few years back. What attracted me was the income potential of the MLM scheme and the quality and integrity of the product (Great slogan: "All of the good, none of the bad."). Many people I know have a similar high regard for the NuSkin product. In fact, I have a neighbor who became so turned on to the shampoos, skin creams and conditioners made by NuSkin that she became a distributor just so she could purchase the product at a distributor's discount.

Ultimately, I dropped out of the organization not long after plunking down several hundred dollars for the starter kit, which included resalable product, a training manual and a set of compelling audio cassettes. The misgivings that led to my departure from NuSkin were fairly standard (I *vaporized,* like most new recruits to the MLM numbers game), and they would probably apply to any other MLM organization that you or I might consider. These misgivings surrounded the following:

1. *Product.* I have no complaints about the quality of the NuSkin line. I just can't relate to *cosmetics* with a great deal of enthusiasm. When it comes to sales, I'm more of an *intangible* sort of person. Besides, the idea of smearing anti-wrinkle cream on total strangers was a little too creepy for me; and I began to question my self-identity as a health and beauty aids purveyor.

2. *Meetings.* To recruit new distributors, it's necessary to organize recruiting sessions at your residence. I don't know about you, but I don't feel all that comfortable with 25 people sitting around the coffee table in my living room until 11 p.m. on a weeknight.

3. *Dependency on others.* I'm fairly confident of my own ability, and I know what my strengths and weaknesses are. And once I'm convinced of the worthiness of a venture, I know I'll work day and night to see it through. But having to deal with a disparate group of others who might lack the drive and commitment to be a success is pretty disconcerting, especially if my income is at stake. I might as well be a manager with a big company if insecurity and supervision hassles are my goals.

4. *Saturation.* The biggest problem with all MLM schemes is that you never know how saturated a given

territory really is. Is the territory just getting established? Or are there distributors who've already fished out the best customers and signed up the most promising recruits?

In many ways, the MLM game is the same sort of crap shoot you'd expect from a chain letter. If you get in first, you win; if you get in last, you lose. MLM promoters will almost always argue that your prospective territory is virgin and has unlimited potential for sales and/or recruiting (if only you work hard enough). But of course, the person who signs you up is busily establishing himself or herself in your territory, competing for your business with a healthy head start.

In truth, there's no way to quantify the exact degree of saturation in your territory, unless it can be proven that there have never been any distributors living within a 50-mile radius of your home. Your agreement to come into the MLM organization represents a supreme act of faith, which, to be fair, is the foundation upon which practically any commission sales activity resides.

If you suspect your territory is indeed oversaturated, then you've got two problems once you become a distributor. First, you'll constantly live in fear that your income potential was dead on arrival; and second, your conscience will take a continual beating from trying to sell new recruits on the idea that *they're* getting into a virgin territory, an issue that already has you worried.

## Making a fair evaluation

I bear no resentment whatsoever for the money I lost on NuSkin. If anything, I was overly enthusiastic in the beginning, and even though the recruiter tried to dissuade me from signing up at the first meeting I went to, I insisted.

In retrospect, I feel the company acted honorably, and I look back on the whole episode as a great learning experience. (My wife and daughter still buy NuSkin products from our neighbor, the consumer/distributor). In another life, maybe it might be my cup of tea, but for this life, the whole thing was clearly a mismatch.

It really annoyed me, though, that Barbara Walters and her ABC news team took a cheap shot at NuSkin on national television, trying to portray the company in a sensational fashion as some sort of evil, exploitive monster, preying on the hopes and fears of thousands of unsuspecting Americans.

True, NuSkin, like many other MLM organizations, hypes the MLM system as a get-rich-quick scheme for anyone with the determination to succeed; and they hammer on the notion that most of us will retire without financial dignity; that the "40-year plan" of working for someone else is a cruel hoax; and that the MLM methodology represents the average person's best hope for reaching financial independence. (Of course, they conveniently sidestep issues such as saturation.)

Whether NuSkin or any other MLM business opportunity crosses the line from legitimacy to scam will always be open to debate, and must be examined on a case-by-case basis. But in my opinion, the MLM method, like the sales rep concept, represents a viable option worthy of consideration.

◆

*In independent selling, there are plenty of opportunities for financial and lifestyle rewards.*

# Chapter 15

———◆———

# Breakaway Options: Franchises and Business Opportunity

———◆———

Here's a question for you: Why waste your time designing a better mousetrap when a perfectly good mousetrap already exists, that you can sell to customers eager to beat a path to your door?

If your answer is, "I don't know," then you may be a candidate for a franchise or business opportunity, ready to ride the coattails of other entrepreneurs who already own the blueprint for a successful operation.

Prepackaged businesses are similar to the bicycle in a box you bought your kid for Christmas. With any luck, all the parts were included, along with a set of instructions and a few simple tools needed to put the thing together.

Provided you were blessed with a modicum of mechanical aptitude, had the ability to follow a plan, and were willing to apply a little elbow grease while your kid was screaming for you to hurry up, the end result was a nice new bike with handlebars in the front, a chain that fit in the sprockets, and a couple of wheels that actually turned when you pushed on the pedals.

Like the bike in a box, a franchise or business opportunity will give you the means to bypass the pitfalls inherent in designing something from scratch that's never been tested and never had the bugs worked out through years of trial and error.

In other words, it can make a lot more sense to read from the sheet music than to play the song by ear.

# 6. Franchises

The popularity and scope of the franchise subculture boggles the mind. According to the International Franchise Association (IFA), franchised businesses racked up more than $716 billion dollars in sales in the U.S. in 1990 alone, with more than *one-third* of all retail sales being generated by franchised operations. Think about it: 102,000 restaurant and fast-food outlets...17,000 convenience stores...11,000 hotels, motels and campgrounds...8,500 tax preparation businesses...

Aside from the household names like Supercuts and Pizza Hut and Chemlawn and Holiday Inn, there are also businesses that few people stop to think about as being franchised; like Miracle Method Bathroom Restoration and Hair Replacement Systems and Balloon Bouquets and The Ultimate Tan and New England Log Homes.

For the record, franchising isn't a business, it's a *method of doing business.* You become a *franchisee* when you enter into an agreement to own and operate a business using the system developed by the *franchisor,* along with the franchisor's name, trademark or service mark.

Franchises offer the entrepreneur many advantages. For example, if the franchisor is well-known, your business will be blessed with name recognition and credibility with customers the instant you hang up a shingle. In most cases, your stationery and business forms will already be designed, your accounting and data processing systems will be in place, your inventory will be on the shelf, and your operations manual will be ready to refer to. Your customers will be familiar with your logo and your methods of operation, and will already be attracted by the advertising and promotion campaign developed by the home office.

By far the most prevalent form of franchising is the *business format* (or "package") franchise, in which, by contractual consent, you buy the right to replicate or "clone" a business from a pre-existing original designed by the franchisor.

Less common are the *trademark* (or "brand name") franchises and *distribution* franchises, in which a proprietary manufacturing process is licensed, or the distribution of goods in a designated territory is granted. Trademark franchises are generally awarded to soft drink bottlers and food processors, while distribution franchisees include gas stations and car dealers.

## The costs (and rewards) of doing business

Franchises and business opportunities share a common goal: to sell you a blueprint that enables you to start a business of your own. There are, however, some important differences worth noting in their respective methods and long-term objectives. (Business opportunities will be discussed in more detail later in this chapter.)

While both vehicles can be of tremendous value, the franchise system represents a more serious, long-term relationship than the business opportunity, which in commercial terms is more like a one-night stand.

When you buy the rights to a franchise, you get the legal license to use the franchisor's trademarks, logos, architectural designs, secret recipes—the whole kit and caboodle.

Franchises generally require a great deal more capital investment than business opportunities; and in return, the franchisor provides training and ongoing support that's proportionately more comprehensive in nature. In fact, most franchisors require the franchisee to follow an unwavering diet consisting of preset marketing plans, operational procedures, quality control standards and so forth, in the hope that a strict regimen of franchise care and feeding will forcibly cause success to occur.

While either system can start you out for as little as a few hundred dollars, *franchising fees* can go as high as $20,000, with additional fixed costs for training. Business opportunities are far less rigid than franchises in the way they're set up, and some give you options as to how much money you need to spend (and how you need to spend it) in order to learn the business and get it off the ground. In some cases, you'll be given choices regarding your exact business relationship with the offeror, and become an "affiliate" or an "associate." Such is the freewheeling nature of business opportunities.

The American Institute of Consumer Credit, a business opportunity out of Miami, Florida, for example, gives you the choice of two different training programs: you can either purchase a home study package containing a set of 10 audiocassettes and a workbook for $200, or you can fork over $10,000 to attend a three-day seminar in Costa Mesa. The choice depends on the perceived value of the training (and the depth of your pockets).

## The ties that bind

Franchisors, of course, have a vital and tangible stake in your success. Unlike business opportunities, they receive ongoing royalties, usually somewhere between 1 percent to 10 percent of sales from the franchisee; and may also receive revenues in the form of service fees from the food, equipment, computer software or operating systems sold or leased to the franchisee. In addition, many franchisors will require you to make a monthly contribution to cover advertising and other cooperative expenses.

Fortunately, franchisors, who have the power to *taketh away*, also have the power to *giveth*. Many franchisors, for example, can help the franchisee cut his or her costs by virtue of the considerable buying power wielded by the parent organization. Jazzercise, for example, offers its franchisees $1 million worth of liability insurance for only $100 a year, which is a fraction of the street price for this type of coverage. In addition, some franchisors offer varying types of financial assistance; a perk not usually provided by the offerors of business opportunities.

With a business opportunity, once you've paid the initiation, equipment and training fees, you're free and clear—a fact that can be viewed as either an advantage or disadvantage, depending on your point of view. Even though the "ongoing support" provided to those who purchase business opportunities generally evaporates after the initial training has been completed, the tradeoff is that you are not continually being pestered by intrusive district managers and home office executives who refuse to take their fingers out of your eyes.

At the other end of the franchise spectrum is the home office that fails to live up to its promise and seems to disappear when training and support are needed the most. Many franchisors make promises that are either insincere or can't be kept for one reason or another, leaving the franchisee wondering what the heck the royalty fees are for.

## Before you strike a deal

There are a number of different kinds of franchise agreements. *Area development* agreements grant the franchisee the right to establish and operate multiple units within a given territory, while *master franchise* agreements allow the franchisee to sub-franchise to other entrepreneurs.

When it comes to agreements and methods, franchisors are regulated by the Federal Trade Commission, and are required by law to supply the prospective franchisee with a prospectus, known in the business as the *Uniform Franchise Offering Circular*, or UFOC, either at the first face-to-face meeting with the franchisor or 10 days before the franchise agreement is to be signed. This disclosure statement contains information on 23 different subjects relevant to the franchisor's legal and financial history, including bankruptcy, profits, losses, territorial restrictions and protections, training, celebrity endorsements, fees, payments, and so forth.

Even though the UFOC will provide you with a lot of useful information, you'd be well-advised to check with a qualified attorney before you make a decision to sign a franchise agreement. And certainly, you should contact at random several of the people whose names appear on the list of current franchisees (a mandatory item on the UFOC report), not necessarily those the franchisor wants you to talk to.

## Finding the right franchise

To find franchises and do some basic research, you can contact the IFA and ask for a membership directory, which will include an associate member's profile, number of outlets and cash investment requirements. Franchise opportunities also appear in magazines such as *Entrepreneur, Inc.,* and *Business Start-Ups,* and you can always attend any of the IFA-sponsored franchising expos that tour from city to city with the express purpose of taking new franchisees into the fold. Once you've made a serious inquiry, your name will find its way on a mailing list. And before you know it, the opportunities will come to you.

To be a member of IFA, franchisors must have been in business for at least two years, be in satisfactory financial condition, have at least 10 individual units, comply with state and federal full disclosure requirements, and have at least a $100,000 net worth.

Newly franchised businesses (those with less than two years of operating history) are ineligible for membership in the IFA, but they may be worth considering. You just have to weigh the benefits and risks inherent in getting in on the ground floor with a wide-open, yet unproven, franchise opportunity.

Industry experts have pegged the "hot" franchises for the '90s as carry-out or home delivery restaurants, temporary help agencies, financial consulting, small business accounting and tax preparation services, maid services, and day-care centers. But of course, experts tend to be trend *followers,* not trend setters. By the time you launch your franchise, the business climate may have changed (or a particular market may have reached a point of saturation).

## Franchise investment requirements

To help prospective franchisees examine the costs of admission, the IFA has published a guide to the industry, in which franchises are divided into 18 broad categories.

*Median total investments* (exclusive of land and new construction costs) range from a low of around $10,000 for a tax preparation service to a high of $1.3 million for a lodging facility.

Remember that the median investment represents the total amount of money you'd need in order to start up the business, whether or not the money ends up in the hands of the franchisor. Typical investment costs might include (in addition to franchise and training fees): leasehold improvements, office supplies and equipment, furniture, utilities, insurance and working capital; plus whatever specific inventory, uniforms or manufacturing equipment you need to buy or lease before your doors can open.

If you feel you've made a mistake shortly after signing an agreement, you should let the franchisor know right away. Many will agree to refund all or a portion of the franchise fee, since there's nothing to be gained by either side by starting a business that's dead on arrival. In fact, many franchise agreements contain a provision that states that a failure to pass the training course entitles the franchisor to cancel the agreement.

*Fig. 15.1: Here's what you need to ante before the cards are dealt.*

---

### FRANCHISE INVESTMENT COSTS

**Under $100,000 Median Investment**
- Accounting, credit collection, general business systems
- Employment services
- Tax preparation services
- Real estate services
- Construction, home improvement, maintenance or cleaning services
- Educational products and services
- Miscellaneous

**From $100,000 to $300,000 Median Investment**
- Restaurants or fast food facilities
- Convenience stores
- Specialty food shops, including ice cream, bakeries and candy stores
- Nonfood products, including home appliances, gifts, hardware and electronics
- Auto products and services
- Recreation, travel and entertainment
- Printing or copying services
- Laundry and dry cleaning
- Equipment and rental services
- Auto and truck rental

**Over $300,000 Median Investment**
- Hotels, motels and campgrounds

---

A key question you should ask yourself when considering a franchise or business opportunity is: Will a prepackaged business ultimately save you money in the long run, or prove to be unnecessarily expensive? Or in other words, are the name recognition, proprietary methodology and training really worth the cost? The rule of thumb is that if 50 percent or more of your total investment money is used to pay fees, and not on the training, equipment or merchandise, you're paying too much.

## 7. Business opportunities

To get a glimpse into the world of business opportunities, take a few minutes to leaf through magazines such as *Entrepreneur* and *Business Start-Ups*. You'll notice that there are a staggering number of different types of business opportunities from which to choose. Businesses currently in vogue include medical claims processing, cleaning services, home inspection and appraising, and utility, telephone, freight and lease auditing.

Many business opportunities are legitimate operations, and will tell you with no reservations that buying a business opportunity is like buying a car, not a chauffeur. That is, the most you can hope to get from the seller is a vehicle that's in decent working order that you can easily learn to drive.

But if the offeror tells you, "Don't worry, we'll be there with you every step of the way, forever and ever," then you know he or she isn't helping you look at the opportunity realistically, and is implying that the vehicle will take you where you want to go without your taking a firm grip on the wheel.

The truth is, if you've got a success mentality and an old-fashioned work ethic, you can probably make a profit from any type of business opportunity—as long as the opportunity's soundly built, and you're given proper instructions on how to make it run.

## Blaming the victim: The ultimate irony

Each of us has a different way to measure success. In my mind, the only reason for going into business is to make a profit. If that's not your goal, then your venture might more accurately be called a hobby. Therefore, if you don't either recover your investment costs or make a living from the business opportunity you choose within a reasonable period of time, you can't really consider the business a success.

Given these criteria, you should be aware of the fact that only 2 or 3 percent of the people who buy into business opportunities ever become successful. They either drop out of the business quickly or spend years struggling just to hang on. I call these people the living dead. Tragically, most of those who quit the business blame themselves for their failure and, in many cases, their blame is justified.

However, scams in the business opportunity world are rampant, so it's not surprising that many entrepreneurs lose their investments to the modern-day version of snake oil hucksters, who are more than eager to separate them from their hard-earned pension funds or corporate severance settlement.

It's not uncommon to be sold a bill of goods, for example, and never even receive the goods you bought. Other complaints against the industry range from misleading advertising to poor product quality to nonexistent support.

## From con artist to consultant

Several types of business opportunities have earned a reputation for sleaze. Near the top of the list are the medical claims processing and auditing businesses.

The award for most shady, though, belongs to the vending machine industry, according to Mark C. Hathaway, president of Jupiter Consulting, Inc., of Indianapolis.

"They'll size you up for how much they think you can spend, and then try to sell you on the 'multiples' idea," says Mark. "The more machines you buy, the more money you can make.

"The only problem is, vending machine companies are notorious for ripping you off. They'll take your five, ten, or 20 thousand dollars and never send you the machines you paid for."

An 18-year veteran of the industry, Mark used to sell all sorts of business opportunities, many of them outright frauds, to unsuspecting victims nationwide—before he went straight.

Much like an ex-convict with a prison record for burglary who's become a highly-paid security consultant, Mark now works on the sunny side of the street. His company provides a service specifically designed to protect opportunity-seeking clients from the scams and swindles epidemic in the trade.

In addition to providing a thorough background investigation of any business opportunity under consideration, Mark will also evaluate an offeror's probability of delivering on its promises, and will negotiate, if possible, a reduction in investment fees.

## Setting up lines of defense

Business opportunity-seekers would do well to heed Mark's insider advice, which is available in his $30 book, *Scam/Rip-off*. Here are a few words of caution to the uninitiated:

- Check with regulatory and policing agencies before you buy. These include the FTC, the state attorney general, the Better Business Bureau and, more recently, the FBI.

- Avoid companies that have a history of not addressing the grievances of offerees or policing agencies.

- Get referrals from other offerees, but not those in your local area. They might try to discourage you from getting into the same business opportunity, thereby eliminating you from potential competition.

- Talk to others who have invested in the same opportunity you're considering. If at least 50 percent of dissatisfied offerees were given a refund, then the business is probably legitimate.

- Ask the offering company for success figures. Look for a 60-percent success rate from the total number of investors. For those who've succeeded in the business, how long did it take for them to earn back their investment?

There are three lines of defense when it comes to investing in a business opportunity. The first line is to simply avoid making the

investment in the first place. The second is to make your purchases from an offeror with a major credit card. That way, you can
get a refund if you're not fully satisfied. If you decide to ship back
any merchandise or materials to the company, remember to make
them sign for any returned goods. Otherwise, they can claim that
they never received them.

Finally, you can make a stink if you feel you've been the victim
of a scam or rip-off. Letters to the offerors can often have a powerful effect, especially if you threaten to take your grievance to the
attorney general, the postal inspector, the FBI or the local newspaper or TV station.

Another option is to hire a lawyer, but often the company
you're fighting will have a fairly airtight defense planned. Remember, if they're engaged in a criminal activity, it's a good bet they've
been through litigation before, and know how to use every trick in
the book to defend themselves. In the long run, fighting them may
prove to be counterproductive. Hopefully, you'll never reach your
third line of defense.

## Telltale signs of sleaze

Turn and burn operators often can be spotted by the way they
present themselves to the public. If you're dealing with a company
for the first time, or you've gone past the initial investigative steps
and are seriously considering a business opportunity, be on the
lookout for the telltale sign of sleaze:

- Phone calls are returned slowly, or not at all.
- Information that was promised is never sent.
- Written materials you receive are difficult to understand.
- Company representatives are uninformed about the offer
  or contradict each other.
- People in departments not on the front line are difficult or
  impossible to reach.
- Sales agents of the opportunity ask you in the first con-
  versation how much you're willing to spend.
- Company spokespeople deny they're selling a business
  opportunity; instead they're "providing training."

When calling a company for information, it can be frustrating to hear a recorded message that only plays back the hype you just read in their ad or saw on their infomercial. And if you do reach a live person on the other end of the line, it can be extremely annoying to be pitched on the business by a salesperson who comes on like a herd of buffalo.

This type of treatment, however, is standard in the industry, and doesn't necessarily mean the offer's no good. Keep trying, and sooner or later, you'll get the information you need.

## The wind beneath your wings

Business opportunity advertisements and sales pitches are designed to play on your fear of loss and/or desire for gain. Accordingly, most of them repeat variations ad nauseam on the following themes:

**Over 90% of all retired Americans will be
forced to live on less than $12,000 a year.**
(Translation: Jump on this opportunity, or you'll die poor.)

and

**Picture yourself in America's hottest money-making
business—being your own boss and having the time,
freedom and money to enjoy life to the fullest!**
(Translation: You can get rich without a lot of work.)

By recognizing these types of pitches for what they are, you can cut through the hype and proceed to gather the more substantial information you need to make an informed decision. By the way, both of the advertising sound-bites above were brought to you by Natural Choice-USA, a giant in the vending machine (excuse me, automatic merchandising) industry.

In a best-case scenario, a franchise or business opportunity will act like the wind beneath the wings of your high-flying business aspirations. The question you need to answer before you invest your time, enthusiasm and hard-earned capital in a pre-packaged business is: Am I getting the wind or just the hot air?

## Buying an existing business

The ultimate business in a box is the one that already exists. For reasons that are fairly obvious, a business that you can buy lock, stock and barrel can be an awfully attractive investment, as long as you don't fall into the trap of buying a lemon, or over-estimating your ability to safely control a horse whose saddle you jumped into while it was in full gallop.

Many former corporate executives make the mistake of buying failing businesses with the assumption that they can turn them around by virtue of their considerable managerial skills, However, the experience gained from climbing the corporate ladder and the experience needed to run a small business are like apples and oranges.

Furthermore, if you happen to buy a business with a bad reputation, you'll have to rebuild your customers' confidence, which may require you to clean house of the existing employees, or totally revamp the inventory.

## Estimating a business' worth

Sometimes it's difficult to estimate the true value of a business. For example, a business might be worth a lot more than it seems because of creative bookkeeping designed to show Uncle Sam as little profit as possible. Some owners tend to skim profits out of the business for their personal use, and "borrow" from the company kitty to pay for things like vacations, cars, and so forth.

By the same token, a company's debt might be greater than it seems on the surface. Therefore, the sale price you agree to should take into consideration the business' existing financial obligations.

For example, if a $50,000 bank loan taken out the previous year becomes your responsibility, the loan amount (as well as any other encumbrances) should be deducted from the purchase price. At the very least, you can fend off legal tangles and give yourself a measure of financial protection in the future by writing a provision into the sales agreement that states that any disputes you and the seller may have after the sale is concluded will be handled by an independent arbitrator, and that both parties waive their right of appeal.

To protect yourself from "surprises" that could put you behind the eightball before the old owner hand over the keys, check for the following not-always-visible problems:

- *Physical damage or deterioration.* Check the building, equipment, furniture and fixtures of the business for hidden (or even obvious) signs of wear or obsolescence.
- *Worthless inventory.* Make sure what you're buying is worth what you're paying. For example, the resumes and customer lists of other headhunters aren't worth the paper they're printed on to me. In service businesses like mine, files and lists have little value by themselves; the real value is in what you make of them.
- *Ailing customer or supplier relationships.* Before you buy a business, make sure a measure of good will already exists between the business and those who'll be critical to its success.
- *"Pending" sales or business growth.* I don't know about you, but I find it hard to put much faith in wishful thinking. Like they say, you can't take "if only," "hopefully," or "any day now" to the bank.
- *Suspicious motives.* Exactly why is the seller trying to unload the business? Is he or she sick and retiring or sick and tired from beating a dead horse?

Before you seriously consider buying a business, check these things out to your satisfaction. And by all means, have you accountant and attorney look over the seller's books very carefully.

## Working with business brokers

Business brokers can be extremely valuable to a buyer, not only for their expertise in locating a business that's for sale, but also for their ability to do the necessary research and legwork that's a prerequisite to putting a deal together. For example, a competent business broker can check into things like tax, title, zoning and parking issues, as well as other nitty-gritty legal and financial details.

Like realtors, business brokers earn a commission from the seller on each concluded transaction. Therefore, they'll be inclined to emphasize the best features of the business, and downplay the worst. Be careful not to put all your trust into the hands of brokers—they have a vested interest in earning a commission, not in making you successful.

Business brokers usually work within the small to medium-sized business realm, and some specialize in certain types of businesses, like restaurants. Truly large transactions involving several millions of dollars are generally the bailiwick of the mergers and acquisitions professionals.

To protect yourself, you can specify in your contract that the broker will sort out all outstanding bills that are the seller's responsibility. If the broker overlooks one, then he or she pays, not you. An honest and conscientious broker will also help educate a novice buyer, and will help put together a deal in which the buyer makes a down payment and finances the rest of the purchase price of over a period of time.

Remember, there are plenty of options when it comes to choosing a breakaway career.

———◆———

*If you decide not to build your own mousetrap, you can always buy a business in a box.*

## Chapter 16

---◆---

# Breakaway Options: Startup, Retail and Restaurant Realities

---◆---

Up until now, we've discussed the various merits and perils of medium- and high-density careers; that is, careers in which you're the central figure or business partner—the person without whom, the venture ceases to exist.

In this final chapter, however, I'd like to talk about low-density careers, ones that are executed through organizations consisting of employees who contribute to your success by playing a variety of roles.

Any type of business or occupation, no matter how small initially, can be expanded into a bigger operation. Even high-density breakaways like writers, freelancers and consultants can hire other people, or enlarge the dimensions of what they do, requiring the help of others to market, sell, distribute, manufacture or administer new products or services offered to the customer.

Some ventures, however, can only be executed with the support of a well-defined organization, and can only experience revenue growth in proportion to the number of employees on staff.

To illustrate this slice of the breakaway option, we'll look at three types of businesses: startups, in which a high-tech product is manufactured; retail operations; and restaurants. These businesses are related not only in regard to the importance of the employee/revenue quotient, but also by the fact that they generally require a good bit of initial and sustained working capital to get off the ground.

# 8. The high-tech startup

Make no mistake: The ultimate objective of a startup is to create a substantial monetary reward for the founder and/or principal officers. As a wealth-generating vehicle, the prototypical startup is a team-oriented business, which, through large infusions of third-party capital, is built into a fast-growing venture that reaches sales revenues of at least $20 million.

The startup script is fairly simple: First, you develop a marketable product. Then, you create a dynamite business plan that you use as a means to round up big-money investors (either venture capitalists or angels) to fund your company's growth. Armed with plenty of cash, you acquire the space, equipment and raw materials (as well as the key managers and employees) you need to grow the business over a period of five years or so.

Finally, you take the company public. Based on the value and the amount of the stock you own in the corporation, you should be able to make a considerable amount of money through the initial public offering (IPO) transaction, perhaps as much as several million dollars.

This wealth-generating scenario should sound like sweet music to any team-oriented entrepreneur's ears. There are, however, a few things you should know before you drop whatever it is you're doing in the hopes of growing a startup business.

First of all, only 10 to 30 percent of startups seriously seeking venture capital ever succeed in getting funded, with only .04 percent of the 700,000 businesses that incorporate each year actually going public.

Secondly, according to Mike Baird in his excellent book, *Engineering Your Start-Up*, an entrepreneur in a venture capital-backed startup has about an even chance of failure, breaking even and becoming wealthy. However, if the company does go public, the founder stands to make about $6.5 million within five years of starting the business.

## Give your startup a fighting chance

Startup success is based on a number of factors. Assuming you have the stamina to put in 50-hour, six-day work weeks without taking a vacation for a few years, (and your immediate family has the fortitude to support your efforts), your business has a fighting chance if you excel in these key areas:

- *Product selection.* Your product must first fill a need or provide an obvious, perceived benefit to the customer. If you can do this through a revolutionary breakthrough in technology, fine. Otherwise, you'll need to establish demonstrable product differentiation in the eyes of the customer.

- *Product positioning.* Your product must compete in the marketplace relative to other products that may be cheaper or of higher perceived quality. The task at hand is to find an untapped niche in which you can clearly gain market share ("hit 'em where they ain't"), or go toe-to-toe with a competitor that you're sure to beat.

- *Product marketing.* Unless the product is customer-driven and has a large enough market potential, no amount of hype will sell it.

- *Profit potential.* Run the numbers. If you can't build enough profit into your product, then what's the point of starting up a company to manufacture it?

- *Product manufacturing.* Let's suppose a scientist friend is urging you to start up a company specializing in the manufacture of computer chips made from Kryptonite. Sounds tempting. The only problem is, that particular substance is in short supply and only a few individuals on the planet know how to deal with its unusual properties.

In all likelihood, a Kryptonite chip would be problematic to manufacture, to say the least. Conversely, a product that's relatively easy to manufacture will ultimately give you the benefit of economies of scale, especially when your company launches similar products in which parts, machinery and processes can be interchanged or cross-utilized.

## 9. Retail peaks and valleys

Compared to the high-tech startup, with its unyielding *modus operandi* of wealth generation, the world of retailing seems very laid-back. There's usually no need for massive amounts of venture capital, you don't have to manufacture anything, and there's no compelling reason to take your company public in five years' time.

However, if you plan to grow your business at all, you'll need to hire employees to run the store in your absence. In fact, that's what you may learn to love about the life of retail; that the store won't fold if you take a long weekend.

Like startups and restaurants, the fortunes of retail shops may rise and fall according to circumstances over which you have no control, such as changes in the economic outlook, fads in the marketplace and oversaturation (or price cutting) by competitors.

Retail stores are also held hostage to seasonal peaks and valleys. Unless you set up shop in a resort or near an attraction that boosts sales independent of the seasonal norms, you'll have to hope that what you earn in the holiday rush between Thanksgiving and Christmas (and during the back-to-school frenzy in late summer) will carry you through the slow period between New Year's and Easter.

## Location, location, location

Before you set up shop, think about what you'd like to sell, not only in terms of what products turn you on, but also in terms of what the traffic will bear in a particular market.

Santa Fe, New Mexico, for example, is the third largest retail art market in the United States, after New York and Chicago. However, the people who buy art in Santa Fe are very particular about what they're looking for.

Ever since the emergence of *Santa Fe style* as a major design trend in the 1980s, hardly anything can be sold in a gallery that isn't obviously dripping with the Santa Fe "look." Sadly, legitimate works of fine art lacking the "look" languish from lack of demand in a town crawling with well-to-do collectors clamoring for images of high desert landscapes, pueblos, coyotes and red chiles that they can schlep back to their living rooms in Chicago, Los Angeles and New York City.

Characterizing the market where you live according to its demographic realities should help you decide what type of merchandise you'll be able to move, and the exact location of where you'll be able to move it. Location, as they say, may be the three most important considerations of a retail business. But unless you can predict with some degree of accuracy whether the foot traffic past your shop consists of actual *buyers,* you may go out of business before your first year's lease expires.

The original McDonald's restaurant, for example, had plenty of traffic. The only problem was, in the early 1940s, McDonald's was an order-from-your-car style drive-in. The "customers" were mostly teen-age boys who filled the parking lot every afternoon, flirting with the teen-age waitresses. Rarely did the teen-agers actually spend any money.

It wasn't until the McDonald brothers decided to standardize the menu and get rid of the drive-in format in 1948 that the restaurant became a huge success. The McDonalds not only latched onto a demographic trend, they positioned their store to serve only those in a position to buy. (Of course, it was Ray Kroc who took the McDonald franchise to the next level of success, but that's another story.)

## Malls, strips and celebrity havens

As you research the potential locations for your shop, consider the different types available:

- *Malls.* These cultural icons are the enclosed shopping centers that are anchored by one or more well-known department stores. Malls will attract customers from a distance of several miles, or from out of town, if the mall is properly positioned or has a compelling theme. The Mall of America in suburban Minneapolis actually contains, in addition to several hundred retail stores, a Knott's Camp Snoopy amusement park complete with roller-coaster rides and a miniature golf course. The advantage to a mall is that there's usually an abundance of foot traffic, thereby eliminating the need for a lot of advertising; and your competition is limited by the management. The downside is that rents are very high, and malls themselves tend to experience their own ups and downs.

- *Neighborhood shopping centers.* These serve a more localized area, and are usually anchored by a supermarket, discount store or home improvement center. In these types of markets, the rents are less, but so is the volume of foot traffic.

- *Retail strip developments.* Known as "strip malls" in the Midwest, these block-long clusters of less than a dozen stores provide retail space for less rent than most malls or shopping centers, and serve a smaller market.

- *Kiosks.* These are small structures located outdoors or in the common areas of a mall. Typically, the rent consists of a portion (usually between 20 and 25 percent) of your gross volume. Although the rent is relatively low and the kiosk is right in the customers' line of sight, kiosk attendants are stuck all day in close quarters. A kiosk can, however, be used as a low-risk proving ground for a larger retail operation.

- *Freestanding stores.* If you can find a storefront in a location that's hot, you can really rock 'n roll, provided crime and parking aren't deterrents to your business. Local zoning laws permitting, you can even turn your home into a store, which can definitely give you certain

201

advantages or disadvantages, depending on your situation. Generally speaking, the more you stray from the beaten path, the more you'll need to spend on advertising.

Speaking of hot locations, I remember when the Melrose Avenue retail district in West Hollywood was just a laid-back, semi-residential conglomerate of wacky boutiques, hardware stores and fish markets, stuck dab smack in the middle of an Orthodox Jewish neighborhood.

In what seemed like the retail equivalent of spontaneous combustion, the Melrose mystique caught fire and the district was transformed practically overnight into a frenzied, trend-setting haven for celebrities, status-seekers and the ultra-rich.

Without a doubt, plenty of old-time Melrose retailers made a fortune from the transition (with the possible exception of the hardware store and fish market owners).

## A checklist for site evaluation

To make sure the location of your retail business suits your needs and offers you a fighting chance of success, evaluate the following factors:

- *Visibility*. Look for locations, especially in malls, that are front and center, not hidden by signs, obstructions, escalators or kiosks.
- *Accessibility*. Choose locations that are near safe parking or are in proximity of other stores. Study the vehicle traffic patterns in the area to make sure that one-way streets, turn signals or medians won't discourage customers from coming to your store.
- *Customer flow patterns*. Position your retail location so it gives you maximum exposure, especially to impulse buyers. Try to avoid getting stuck in the dead zone of a mall or the end of a one-way street.
- *Competitive interaction*. Cozy up next to other stores that look like they'll complement your business, not detract from it. A Bible store, for example, would be better situated next door to a church, rather than a head shop.

- *Store personality.* Allow yourself the opportunity for self-expression. If you feel a large sign visible from the highway, for example, will help attract passers-by, then don't lease retail space restricted by a city ordinance prohibiting outdoor advertising.

- *Compatibility.* Familiarize yourself with some of the other merchants in the area you're considering, to see if you're welcome.

  The last thing you want is to feel antagonism from your new neighbors, especially when cooperation on issues such as zoning, building inspection, sanitation and crime control is clearly in the collective self-interest. If the merchants belong to an association, find out if you can sit in on a meeting; or if they publish a cooperative advertising circular, study it to get a feel for the way they relate to their markets.

## Getting your retail business started

The amount of inventory you need to carry should be your first consideration. Naturally, there'll be a great deal of difference in the number of units needed to open a shop that sells vintage guitars in the $2,000 to $15,000 price range than the amount needed to run a discount linen store in which the average retail price is $10 per item.

In either case, though, you should start off by buying "broad and shallow," or in other words, buy a lot of variety, but not a lot of duplication. You can always order more of what you need later; but you'll never know what's popular with your customers until you give them the chance to choose between a wide variety of items on the shelf.

Every type of retail business has its own formula, simple or complex, that's used for the purpose of merchandise planning. For example, in the retail T-shirt business, the equation is:

$$maximum\ sales\ volume \div turnover \div average\ selling\ price =$$
$$the\ number\ of\ units\ of\ merchandise.$$

*Turnover* refers to the number of times you sell your inventory over the course of a year. In the T-shirt business, a turnover rate of six times a year is considered good.

For the specific products you plan to sell, check with a sales rep or merchandising consultant to make sure you apply the correct formula, and don't get in over (or under) your head when it comes to stocking inventory.

Over-buying will tie up your cash, 10 or 15 percent of which should be kept in reserve for filling in sold-out inventory or investing in new merchandise that you discover to be hot. As time goes by, you can make buying decisions based on your store's sales history and customer preferences. If you categorize your merchandise, you can allocate the percentage of shelf space you give each product category relative to its past performance.

By establishing an inventory control system, you can analyze buying patterns and standardize your accounting and reordering procedures. An inventory control system can be as simple as using tear-off price tags bearing duplicate stock numbers and price information; or as complex as a computerized bar coding system that tracks inventory, manages cash flow, accumulates and crunches product/customer data, and automatically reorders new merchandise.

# A reptile approach to fixtures

Aside from inventory, a retailer needs to work intelligently with *fixtures*, a broad term that defines everything in the store (and in the window), from lighting to props to display cases to furniture to interior design.

Fixtures not only showcase the merchandise to the customer in an appealing manner, they also help create an atmosphere that puts the customer in the mood to buy. Fixtures play an important role in retailing, and help differentiate Retail Store A from Retail Store B, even if the merchandise in the two stores is exactly the same.

Going back to Melrose Avenue, one of my favorite stores a few years back was a trendy menswear shop. What made the store unique was that in the front window and right on the middle of the

floor were giant glass terrariums, each containing a bevy of miniature live alligators.

The *ambiance*, I admit, was a bit unusual; but one thing's for
sure: Everyone I knew had either heard of the store or had been
there themselves. While I'm not suggesting you should adopt a
*reptile* theme for your retail establishment, I can tell you that the
intelligent (or imaginative) use of fixtures can have a powerful
impact on your business.

## Advertising, promotion and sales

To advertise and promote your store, you can try every trick in
the book, from yellow pages ads to newspaper, billboard and display ads; from TV and radio spots to coupons, contests and giveaways; from grand openings and after-Christmas clearances to
founder's day anniversary sales; and from press releases and
media placement to direct mail and door-to-door samplers.

Here's a novel approach to advertising and sales. A furniture
store in my home town prides itself on its "everyday low prices."
Therefore, they never, *ever* have a sale. They simply don't need to.
Besides, a sale would undermine the credibility of their standard
low-price policy.

Now, I'm not going to accuse them of stretching the truth. But
I do find it interesting that every six months, the store advertises
a huge "semi-annual factory-authorized inventory reduction
event." But they never have a sale.

Word-of-mouth referrals are the most powerful form of advertising. By providing good service and attentive in-store response to your customers, you'll earn a reputation that will pay
handsome dividends and bring in new and repeat business.

Always keep your cool when dealing with the public. Retailers
say that it takes 10 new customers to overcome the damage done
to your reputation by one unhappy customer.

Good selling skills are another essential ingredient to retail
success. Your goal when selling is threefold: First, you want to
genuinely satisfy the customer; second, you want to close the sale;
and third, you want to capitalize on the opportunity to boost your
profits by selling as much as you can to each individual customer.

## Accessorizing the customer

Back in high school, when I worked as a clerk at a ladies shoe store, I learned the value of maximizing every purchase by either cross-selling merchandise of equal value ("Those shoes look great on you. How're you fixed for pumps?"), or "accessorizing" the sale by showing the customer a selection of accessories, such as matching handbags or belts.

Heck, why stop there? I'd even ask the customer if she could use shoe polish, socks and stockings (I'm dating myself—pantyhose hadn't been invented in 1966). As far as I could tell, the best customer was the one I just made a sale to. And the more I sold, the more commission I earned.

The point is, it takes very little additional effort to strike while the iron is hot. Unfortunately, many retail sales clerks and their managers overlook this vital income-building technique.

Accessorizing is done all the time. The trick is to do it subtly, so the customer feels he or she is getting better service. As we all know, nothing turns the customer off more than a high-pressure sales clerk.

Waiters and waitresses, who are the eatery equivalent to sales clerks, are trained to ask whether you want a cup of coffee or a low-fat dessert after your meal. They're accessorizing you, just like any motivated sales professional would. They know where the real profit is.

## 10. The restaurant reality

Restaurants, like startups and retail shops, can also provide a terrific vehicle for wealth generation—or, for that matter, physical exhaustion.

Luckily, the restaurant trade offers alternatives to the full-service eat-in model, in which your personal presence is either required or on-call 24 hours a day, seven days a week. There are many types of specialty eateries now that cater to the business, breakfast or weekend crowd; so if you feel the need to fill a part-time niche, there's plenty of opportunity.

Like retailing, the restaurant trade is incredibly competitive, especially from franchise restaurant and fast-food operations whose home offices have no qualms about spending zillions of dollars on advertising and promotion.

However, the personal touch is one of the qualities that customers are warming up to today, especially in the age of comfort food and gorilla-sized portions. If your restaurant provides good food at a reasonable price and can distinguish itself from the predictability of the chains, then you've got a real shot at success. Unique or different themes are more popular now than ever, so a trendy idea for a Cuban cafeteria, a Renaissance road house or a log cabin lunchroom might very well attract a large and loyal following.

If your restaurant theme idea is strong enough, you can either accessorize or cross-sell your customers on catering services or related merchandise. I've never been to an historic restaurant, for example, that didn't attempt to sell *faux* antiques in its gift shop, or a Bob Evans that didn't display tacky trinkets and take-home syrups by the cash register. By the same token, the T-shirts sold by the Hard Rock Cafes around the world seem to have reached the same annoying level of ubiquity as the *smiling faces* of the 1970s. But that's free enterprise for you.

## Cash considerations

Even if the food and atmosphere are all you've got to sell, there's plenty of money to be made in the restaurant business. Startup costs will vary, of course, depending on the location, style and seating capacity of your restaurant, as well as the cost of land, leasing, equipment, furnishings and renovation.

Income, too, is dependent on a variety of factors, including the daily volume of customer flow and the average price (and profit) of the meals you serve. Here are a few examples of the numbers you can expect from a restaurant of 100 seats, according to the editors of *Entrepreneur Magazine:*

**Pizzeria**
Average net profit before taxes:      $87,000
Minimum startup costs:                $97,000

**Salad Bar Restaurant**
Average net profit before taxes:         $115,000
Minimum startup costs:            $73,000

**Coffee Shop**
Average net profit before taxes:         $73,000
Minimum startup costs:            $85,000

To estimate your yearly gross income, start with the daily gross and multiply this figure by the number of days you expect to operate in a week times the number of weeks you expect to operate in a year.

For example, if you have:

*20 tables x 5 meals x $9 = $900 daily gross income,*

then this can be extrapolated into

*$900 x 6 days x 48 weeks = $259,200 yearly gross income.*

The conventional wisdom is that you should go into business with as large a restaurant as you can afford. The reasoning is that a 100-seat coffee shop requires only a few thousand dollars more to set up than a 50-seater; but the profit potential of a 100-seater is obviously much greater.

# And finally: Serving the public

Aside from the administrative headaches you'll suffer in the form of paperwork, taxes, workers' comp and insurance, you'll also need to deal with the generally transient and unprofessional nature of restaurant help. Therefore, a competent, career-oriented chef or bartender can be a tremendous asset to your business, so it's worth the extra cost to get a pro on the team.

It goes without saying that whenever you open your doors to the public, you stand the chance of being patronized by drunks, thieves, indigents, militant anti-smokers, obnoxious political extremists, tip-scrooges and every other imaginable type of ill-mannered whiner-diner.

However, owning a restaurant also gives you the opportunity to participate in truly worthwhile and meaningful community activities. Jim Tarbell, the owner of Arnold's restaurant in Cincinnati, works tirelessly to improve the quality of his city, and generously donates the use of his facilities to charitable organizations, literary societies, art guilds and community development groups.

Like any low-density breakaway career, there are a lot of stresses involved in managing an organization and putting its care and feeding above your own personal needs. But the rewards of running a startup, restaurant or retail store can be considerable, and represent just a few of the many ways you can find happiness and financial success by being your own boss.

———◆———

*Good luck and bon appetite*
*in your new breakaway career!*

# Chapter 17

◆

# Breakaway Career Resources

◆

There are countless numbers of resources for breakaways. And one of the best places to find them is your nearby public, college, government or business library. In nearly every chapter of *Breakaway Careers,* I've referred to specific sources of information, which appear in greater detail here. I've also included additional books, magazines, newsletters, trade associations, government agencies and universities whose information and guidance can put you on the path toward higher breakaway education.

As I mentioned in the introduction, my goal is to help you evaluate potential opportunities and give you the skills you need to run your business in a competitive market. It's unlikely that any one resource can answer all your questions; so please, learn as much as you can about the career of your choice before you venture forth. You'll be glad you did.

## Books

**The 50 Best Low Investment High-Profit Franchises.** Robert Laurance Perry, Prentice Hall.

**The Action Guide to Government Grants, Loans, and Giveaways.** George Chelekis, Putnam Publishing Group.

**American Marketing Association's Complete Guide to Small Business Marketing.** Kenneth J. Cook, NTC Business Books.

**An Introduction to Business Brokerage:** Valuing, Listing and Selling Businesses. C.D. Peterson, John Wiley & Sons, Inc.

**Best Home Businesses of the '90s**: The Inside Information You Need to Know to Select a Home-based Business. Paul and Sarah Edwards, Jeremy P. Tarcher.

**Ecopreneuring:** The Complete Guide to Small Business Opportunities From the Environmental Revolution. Steven J. Bennett, John Wiley & Sons, Inc.

**Engineering Your Start-up**: A Guide for the Hi-Tech Entrepreneur. Michael L. Baird, Professional Publications, Inc.

**Entrepreneur Business Guides.** Entrepreneur Magazine, 800-421-2300. Book sells for $59.50, disk for $19.95, both for $69.50. Contains vital facts, figures and formulas for business owners, with more than 165 types of businesses profiled.

**The Entrepreneurial PC Series** (including Health Service Businesses on Your Home-based PC, Rick Bezel). Windcrest Books, McGraw Hill, Inc.

**The Entrepreneur's Guide to Capital:** Over 150 Proven Ways to Finance New & Growing Businesses. Jennifer Lindsey, Probus Publishing Co.

**Financial Essentials for Small Business Success:** Accounting, Planning and Record Keeping Techniques for a Healthy Bottom Line. Jeff Slater and Joe Tabet, Upstart Publishing.

**Getting Business to Come to You**: Everything You Need to Know to Do Your Own Advertising, Public Relations, Direct Mail and Sales Promotion and Attract All the Business You Can Handle. Paul and Sarah Edwards with Laura Clampitt Douglas, Jeremy P. Tarcher.

**The Great American Idea Book**: How To Make Money From Your Ideas. Bob Coleman and Deborah Neville, W.W. Norton & Co.

**Growing a Business.** Paul Hawken, Simon & Schuster, Inc.

**The Handbook of Small Business Valuation Formulas.** Valuation Press.

**How to Build Sales with Manufacturers' Agents.** Jim Gibbons, Prentice Hall, $59.95.

**How to Look It Up Online.** Alfred Glossbrenner, St. Martin's Press.

**How to Organize and Operate a Small Business.** Clifford M. Baumback, Ph.D., Prentice Hall, Inc.

**How to Really Create a Successful Business Plan.** David E. Gumpert, Inc. Publishing.

**Making It On Your Own**: Surviving the Ups and Downs of Being Your Own Boss. Sarah and Paul Edwards, Jeremy P. Tarcher.

**Own Your Own Franchise.** Ray Baird and Sheila Henderson, Addison-Wesley Publishing Co.

**Restaurant Industry Operations Report.** National Restaurant Association.

**The Start-up Business Plan.** William M. Luther, Prentice Hall Small Business Guide.

**Working From Home**: Everything You Need to Know About Living and Working Under the Same Roof. Paul and Sarah Edwards, Jeremy P. Tarcher.

# Associations and organizations

**American Business Management Association.** Box 111, West Hyannis Port, MA   02672, 508-790-4567 (Business, tax and financial planning services for small and home-based business.)

**American Entrepreneurs Association.** 2392 Morse Ave., Irvine, CA 92714, 714-261-2325.

**Women's Economic Development Corporation (AWED).** 71 Vanderbilt Ave., 3rd Floor, New York, NY   10169, 800-222-AWED (Advice and workshops for women business owners.)

**Center for Family Business.** Box 24268, Cleveland, OH   44124, 216-442-0800.

**Direct Marketing Association.** 11 W. 42nd St., New York, NY   10036, 212-768-7277.

**International Franchise Association.** 1350 New York Ave. N.W., Ste. 900, Washington, DC  20005, 202-628-8000.

**Manufacturers' Agents National Association.** P.O. Box 3467, Laguna Hills, CA  92654-3467.

**National Association for the Cottage Industry.** Box 14850, Chicago, IL 60614, 312-472-8116.

**National Association of Entrepreneurs.** 1400 W. 64th Ave., Denver, CO 80221, 303-426-1166.

**National Association of Home-based Businesses.** P.O. Box 30220, Baltimore, MD 21270, 410-363-3698.

**National Association for the Self-Employed.** 9151 Grapevine Highway, North Ridgeland Hills, TX 76180, 817-656-6313.

**National Business Incubation Association.** 1 President St., Athens, OH 45701, 614-593-4331. (Guide to business "incubators" run by non-profit corporations designed to help start-ups get off the ground by providing low rent, business and financial advice.)

**National Federation of Independent Business.** 600 Maryland Ave. S.W., Ste. 700, Washington, DC 20024, 202-554-9000.

**National Restaurant Association.** 1200 17th St. N.W., Washington, DC 20036, 202-331-5900.

**National Retail Merchants Association.** 100 West 31st St., New York, NY 10001.

**National Small Business United.** 1155 15th St. N.W., Ste. 710, Washington, DC 20005, 202-293-8830.

**The Small Business Network.** 1341 Ancona Drive, La Verne, CA 91750, 800-825-8286 (A knowledge network of professionals.)

**Small Business Administration (SBA).** 409 Third St. S.W., Washington, DC 20416, 800-827-5722 (The primary source of federal assistance for small business owners.)

- **Answer Desk Hotline.** Call 800-827-5722 for recording on available resources and many topics.
- **Mentor Program.** A mentoring program for women business owners who are ready to expand their businesses.
- **Small Business Development Centers.** Located on about 700 college campuses in all 50 states, they offer counseling on financial, marketing and technical areas.
- **Service Corps of Retired Executives (SCORE).** A network of 13,000 retired business executives and professionals volunteer their services on the spot or indefinitely. Low cost business management seminars are also available.

- **Small Business Institutes.** Centers on some 500 university and college campuses offer free guidance from a senior business administrator and marketing students.

**U.S. Chamber of Commerce.** 1615 H St. N.W., Washington, DC 20062, 202-463-5580 (Small Business Center and publications and programs.)

**U.S. Government Printing Office.** 202-783-3238 (Offers a broad range of free publications.)

## Resources for education

**Bear's Guide to Earning Nontraditional College Degrees.** Ten Speed Press.

**Entrepreneur Magazine's Business Guides.** 800-421-2300.

**Entrepreneurial Studies Program.** Babson College, One College Drive, Babson Park, MA 02157, 617-235-1200 (Conferences and Entrepreneurs Hall of Fame.)

**The Foundation Center.** 79 Fifth Avenue, New York, NY 10003, 212-620-4230 (Seminars on grant writing.)

**National Home Study Council (NHSC).** 1601 18th St. N.W., Washington, DC 20009, 202-234-5100.

**Resources for Entrepreneurship Education.** Occupational Curriculum Laboratory, East Texas State University, Commerce, TX 75428, 903-886-5623 (A range of vocational programs.)

**School of Business Administration.** Entrepreneur Program, University of Southern California, Bridge Hall Room 6, Los Angeles, CA 90089-1421, 213-740-0641.

## Directories and resource guides in your library reference section

**Bacon's.** Bacon's Publishing Company, Inc. (Comprehensive resource on publicity.)

**Business Organizations and Agencies Directory.** Gale Research Co.

**Directory of Business, Trade and Public Policy Organizations.** Small Business Administration.

**Directory of Publications.** Gale Research Co.

**Encyclopedia of Associations.** Gale Research Co.

**Federal Database Finder.** Information USA, Inc.

**Franchise Annual Directory.** Info Franchise News.

**Franchising Opportunities.** International Franchise Association.

**Macmillan Guide to Correspondence Study.** Macmillan Publishing Co.

**Mancuso's Small Business Resource Guide.** Joseph R. Mancuso, Prentice Hall Press.

**Minority Information Resources Directory.** TRY US Resources, Inc.

**NUCEA Guide to Independent Study Through Correspondence Instruction.** Peterson's Guides.

**Small Business Index: Volume 2.** Wayne D. Kryszak, The Scarecrow Press.

**Small Business Sourcebook.** Gale Research Co.

**Standard Directory of Advertising Agencies.** National Register Publishing.

**Standard Rate & Data Service (SRDS).** (Advertising rates and information for periodicals.)

**Trade Shows Worldwide.** Gale Research Co.

# Magazines and newsletters

*Agency Sale.* Manufacturers' Agents National Association, P.O. Box 3467, Laguna Hills, CA 92654-3467, 714-859-4040 (Published monthly, subscription price $37.50 per year.)

*Business Start-ups.* Entrepreneur Magazine Group, Box 57050, Irvine, CA 92619.

*Cottage Connection.* P.O. Box 14850, Chicago, IL 60614 (Issues and trends of interest to home-based business owners.)

*Entrepreneur Magazine.* Box 57050, Irvine, CA 92619.

*Home Office Computing.* 441 Lafayette St., New York, NY 10003.

*In Business.* JG Press, Inc., 419 State Ave., Emmanus, PA 18049.

*Inc.* 38 Commercial Wharf, Boston, MA 02110.

*Journal of Small Business Management.* National Council for Small Business Management and the Small Business Development Center, Box 6025, West Virginia University, Morgantown, WV 26506.

*NASBIC News.* National Association of Small Business Investment Companies (NASBIC), 512 Washington Blvd., Washington, DC 20005 (News of government activity of concern to small businesses seeking capital).

*The Newsletter on Newsletters.* The Newsletter Clearinghouse, 44 W. Market St., Box 311, Rhinebeck, NY 12572.

*Success Magazine.* 230 Park Ave., New York, NY 10169, 212-551-9500.

*The Wall Street Journal.* "Business Opportunities" Section.

# Online services

**CompuServe Information Service.** Online videotext service including The Computer Consultant's Forum, The Computer Training Forum, The Working Home Forum, 800-848-8199.

**Entrepreneur's Forum.** A service of CompuServe and *Entrepreneur Magazine*, free to CompuServe subscribers, 800-421-2300.

**Time-Place.** On online database of seminars conducted by more than 6,000 providers, 617-890-4636.

# About the Author

Bill Radin is a graduate of the University of Southern California School of Music and the University of Cincinnati's College Conservatory of Music. He began his career in executive search in 1985, where he became training director and manager of sensor technologies for Search West in Los Angeles and training director and department manager of Management Recruiters in Cincinnati. His clients include Eaton Corporation, TRW, Ciba Geigy, NEC America and Emerson Electric, as well as dozens of small- to medium-sized high-tech companies specializing in sensor research, development and manufacturing.

Bill is the author of the books *Take This Job and Leave It, Billing Power! The Recruiter's Guide to Peak Performance,* and *The Recruiter's Almanac of Scripts, Rebuttals and Closes.* His articles have appeared in a number of trade publications, including *SENSORS, Weighing & Measurements* and *Personnel Consultant* magazines. Originally from Alexandria, Virginia, Bill lives in Santa Fe, New Mexico with his wife, Ruth, and stepdaughter Randi.

# Index